a life...
well,
lived.

a life... well, lived.

RAY WYLIE HUBBARD

with THOM JUREK

a life... well, lived.

Inquiries should be addressed to

Bordello Records
PO Box 2706
Wimberly, TX 78676

Cover photograph by Judy Hubbard

Photo design by Javi Garcia

Photos by Ron McKeown or used with permission from author

Written with Thom Jurek

Afterword first published 2011 in *Lone Star Music Magazine*

ISBN 978-0-9861125-0-8 PBK
ISBN 978-0-9861125-1-5 HBK

Printed in the United States of America
at OneTouchPoint/Ginny's Printing in Austin, Texas

He who learns must suffer. And even in our sleep,
pain that cannot forget falls drop by drop upon the heart,
and in our own despair, against our will,
comes wisdom to us by the awful grace of God.
— Aeschylus

Some get spiritual 'cause they see the light
and some 'cause they feel the heat.

— Judy Hubbard

foreword

i remember seeing a movie about a wild young folk singer who left a trail of scorched earth behind him as he traveled from texas to colorado singing songs and drinking beer and goofing off mostly, not wanting for nothing except a new set of guitar strings and true love...at least for a night...and meeting poets and artists and cowboy character actors and motorcycle racers and one time drinking homemade wine with an honest to god real gypsy who had a huge scar running from his shoulder to his chin he had gotten in a knife fight with a soldier over a gypsy princess in hungary (she later died in the revolution and he never fell in love again) and running with young powerful performers named steven fromholz, dan mccrimmon, johnny vandiver, big bill moss, allen damron, michael murphey (before he added his middle name of martin), charles lewis stevenson III who became buckwheat stevenson and then b.w. stevenson and rick fowler, wayne kidd, and an old blues cat named mance lipscomb, and so many other just flat out cool wanderers cast upon the earth sharing a common thread of caring about and encouraging one another while on their travels here...and how one night he rode an old motorbike without a headlight from red river n.m. to angel fire n.m. to see a girl who was leaving the next day and somewhere about one o'clock in the morning, grateful there was a full moon lighting up the highway, realized he wasn't in love but was just a horny dumb ass on a motorcycle without a headlight on a highway in the sangre de christo mountains and...and...wait...aw man, that wasn't a movie...it was my old head remembering stuff. sorry.

rwh

so here's the part of the book that i skip when i read other books. do i really wanna read that some author thanks his 3rd grade school teacher? i mean i had some good teachers but i also had a couple of teachers who were dicks. instead of thanking people here maybe i should make a list of the people i owe an apology to…probably. but as it stands i do want to thank some people cause if i do win some award, i'm sure the music will start before i'm finished so i'm gonna do it here and you can start the cut off music and go to the next page anytime you want.

first and foremost there's judy, who walks like a stripper, meditates like a monk, works like a brain surgeon, laughs like a flower if it could laugh, keeps the machine oiled and running and is the woman i love.

my son lucas who earned the gig, it is an honor to share the stage with him every time.

my son cory who deserves his happiness.

thom jurek who insisted on and inspired me to do this, and writes from that place only the true poets know.

here's a list of people i wanna thank but i ain't gonna write why i'm thanking them…i'm just gonna thank 'em: my mom, helen and my dad, royce and my grandpas and grandmas, jack, earl, tilda, and annie.

also to mattson rainier, josh jones, jeremy tepper, sam swank, richard skanse, gurf morlix, lloyd maines, george reiff, troy campbell, rick richards, hayes carll, kyle schneider, brent carpenter, joe & marjorie walsh, richard starkey, ronnie dunn, rick fowler, terry ware, tony joe white, charlie musselwhite, chris robinson, dr. don johnston, jerry jeff walker, pat toomay, stephen king, john stanford, logan bosemer, elizabeth cook, david letterman, jimmy fallon, conan o'brien, tony nobles (exception: for what he does to my guitars), charlie solomon, gibson guitars, south austin music, charlie's guitars, thirty tigers, estes audiology,

and those who are no longer here but helped me along the way: stevie ray vaughan, charles palmer, bugs henderson and duke roberts.

and last but certainly not least…god, as i understand him/her/whatever….or even if i don't understand the concept at all.

contents

The Messenger

Written by Ray Wylie Hubbard
Snake Farm Publishing (SESAC)

I am wearing old boots with high Cuban heels
Our souls they are worn and we stand here by grace
My trousers are torn and my jacket is borrowed
I am wearing my time behind the eyes in my face

I am not looking for loose diamonds
Or pretty girls with crosses around their necks
I don't want four roses and water
I am not looking for God
I am not looking for sex

I've worn out my welcome in certain small circles
In Spanish bordellos and Confederate states
But there is an angel in leathers and kindness
Who whispers my name and smiles at my fate

All the true believers are out on the road tonight
And no matter what happens, you know they'll be okay
And to the rock and roll gypsies, may the last song you sing
Be by Mr. Van Zandt if you're ever in old Santa Fe

Now I have a mission and a small code of honor
To stand and deliver by whatever measures
And the message I give you is by this old poet
He said our fears are like dragons guarding our most
precious treasures

I am not looking for loose diamonds
Or pretty girls with crosses around their necks
I don't want four roses and water
I am not looking for God
I just want to see what's next

rwh

jimmy fallon comes into the green room and introduces himself to my son lucas, billy cassis, george reiff, rick richards, my wife judy and me. he was kind, gracious, funny and just plain cool. he thanks us for being on the show and asks if we need anything. i tell him we're okay and that i saw the previous week's show with the rolling stones and how funky it was.
he told me it was exciting, yet pretty intense.
i said having keith and mick on was kinda like you had some vintage rolls royces on last week and tonight you've got a 1984 plymouth station wagon with a trailer hitch, that burns oil, has a piece of cardboard stuffed in the passenger window and red duct tape for the tail lights.
he looked at me and said your album is a rolls. i love it.
i said i had a lot of help.
how this all happened was i was on my way to chicago to play schuba's when judy calls me and said, you're on jimmy fallon! actually, she screamed it like the time she opened the royalty check i got from rapper lloyd banks for the co-write i got on warrior.
lucas gets on the phone.
i said cool, huh?
you're 17 and going to be on national tv.
he said i think i'm gonna get me some alligator shoes.
i say why you gonna do that?
he said don't you think if muddy or lightnin' was going to be on tv, that they'd go buy a new pair of alligator shoes?
i say probably.
when lucas was 14 some guys at his school said they had heard he played guitar and wanted him to join their band. he asked what kind of music they played.
they said soundgarden, nirvana, and stone temple pilots — they had some pretty good paying gigs coming up too.
lucas said, sorry, i'm a bluesman.
then i remembered that the last time i was on national tv it was in 1970. i was bachelor number two on the dating game. my television career was...well...i never had one. i wasn't picked by the girl who modeled panty hose for the jc penney catalog and the consolation prize was an h.i.s. combo suit with 2 reversible vests. i think i wore it once to the saxon pub and got laughed at.

rwh

during the run-though, the guy who does stand in for jimmy introduces me as texas country songwriter — ray wylie hubbard.
i reveal this to judy after soundcheck.
she says this will not stand.
now at one time it was a cool badge to wear — to be known as a texas songwriter because it used to mean you were a reinforced-steel-concrete-honest-to-god-walking-badass-songwriting-son-of-a-bitch - who wasn't metaphor deficient, had read the grapes of wrath, knew that townes van zandt believed song lyrics should stand on their own without music and no matter how bad your twang was, you were literate. once it meant you were mentored by a tradition. nowadays here in texas it means you can get a guitar, steal progressions from a mid-tempo '80s bad big hair rock band from the mtv era, write cliché lyrics, wear your ball cap backwards, stand in a field for your cd cover and have your fraternity brother who has 30 laminates on a lanyard sell your merch...and make some big bucks doing it.
more on this later.
let's get back to the fallon show.
as usual, judy has prophesied. the texas country songwriter thing doesn't stand. at show time, jimmy introduced me as an americana songwriter and recording artist.
during camera rehearsal it was just us and the crew. on the real thing we came out and there are these people behind us on rafters and stairs to the sides and our drummer rick counts the tempo off and these nice, but obviously rhythm-impaired human beings cannot keep time. they start waving their hands in the air, dancing and clapping without regard to any downbeat whatsoever. it sounded like a flock of about 50 seagulls taking off.
okay, but it's just me and my acoustic guitar at the beginning for the whole first verse. the full drum kit, bass, and both electric guitars (through vox ac 30s) don't come in until the chorus. pretty much all we can hear onstage are these handclaps all over the place completely out of sync with the song. imagine the sound of the bats coming out from under the congress street bridge in austin at dark.

rwh

questlove, drummer for house band the roots, actually stands up and graciously starts clapping in time over his head to try and get them together. it doesn't work, they are still clapping completely out of time.

the guys i got are so good that even though they couldn't hear my guitar they came in right on the downbeat of the chorus in spite of hearing what sounded like a box of lincoln logs being dumped out on a linoleum floor.

not only did we not fuck up, we made some good rock.

oh yeah, it was fashion week in new york and somehow people knew we weren't in town for that.

Drunken Poet's Dream

Written by Ray Wylie Hubbard
Snake Farm Publishing (SESAC) and
Hayes Carll Highway 87 Music (SESAC)
Used with Permission

I got a woman who's wild as Rome
She likes being naked and gazed upon
She crosses a bridge then sets it on fire
She lands like a bird on a telephone wire

I'm gonna hollar, I'm gonna scream
I'm gonna get me some mescaline
Then I'm gonna rhyme that with gasoline
It's a drunken poet's dream

There's some money on the table and a pistol on the floor
A few paperback books by Louis L'Amour
Whisky bottles are scattered like last night's clothes
Cigarettes, papers and Oreos

My harmonica's got a busted reed
My lips are chapped and are about to bleed
She says that's nothing when she was a kid
She danced with the Dead at the pyramids

Now I'll never pay back my student loan
Smelling like Coors and cheap cologne
She tells me not to worry about Judgment Day
She says dying to get to Heaven's just not our way

chapter 1

Oklahoma, Blood, God, Pacts

One of my earliest memories is standing on my grandmother's porch when I was five or six. My cousin Billy was 30 feet or so walking away from me. I had a rock the size of an egg in my hand, and for some reason I can't remember, I threw it at him. At that moment, he turned around to yell at me, and I hit him square in the forehead. Blood spurted everywhere. He started screaming and crying and running in circles and then fell to the ground and started rolling around.

My grandmother came out of the house — and by now I was crying — I thought I had killed him. And I prayed: "Oh Lord, if you let him live, I will go to church every Sunday for five years without missing a single day."

My grandmother took him inside and cleaned him up and when I realized he was going to live, I was both relieved and worried, because I knew I was going to get a spanking from my father and my cousin was going to knock the tar out of me when he got the chance. The thought crossed my mind that I'd be better off if he had died. There was a chance he probably would have lived anyway, without my bargaining with the Almighty, but a deal was a deal. For five years, I went every Sunday, no matter what.

Now I had been to Sunday school before, so I was aware of God and Adam and Eve and Noah and the Ark and David and Goliath, and Jesus in the manger and him walking on the water and coming back to life after being dead for a while. I had told my mama about the deal, so off we went that next Sunday along with my grandmother to start my payment plan. My mama hadn't been a big churchgoer before, but now seemed intrigued by the idea.

For some reason this small wooden Baptist church in Soper, Oklahoma, that held maybe 50 people or so, came across this time as a big, scary, loud and dangerous place. I knew I was going to have to go down to the front when they asked sinners to come on down and be saved. I had almost killed someone, so I definitely qualified.

On this particular Sunday, the preacher got to praying and yelling and reading from the Bible and screaming to high heaven for the Lord to save these wretched souls in Southeastern Oklahoma for an hour, then an hour-and-a-quarter.

By now I had to pee and was squirming in my seat and holding my legs together and wondering if he was ever going to quit. Then finally, at the hour-and-a-half point, he said, "Come on down and be saved and be baptized in the name of the Lord." I was sweating and scared and had to pee the worst I can remember. I got up and walked down to the front of the church with everybody singing, "Just As I Am, I Come, I Come."

I got down there and the preacher asks me if I believe and was I ready to have my sins washed away, and I nodded my head. He hands me over to another man and we go behind the podium to this room, and I put on this white robe with just my underwear on, and we go into this big tin vat full of water behind the choir. The preacher now has a robe on and is standing waist deep in the tank. The people are all singing and I see my grandmother and my mama in the pews, and they're crying and waving their arms up in the air.

Then the preacher grabs me and says, "In the name of the Father, the Son and the Holy Ghost, I baptize you." He places one hand behind my back and his other on my forehead and pushes me backward. As I go under the water, I think, "Lord, don't let me pee now, please. Please Lord, just let me hold it," and then I'm underwater and about to cry. I am in so much pain 'cause I've never held it this long and when I come up out of the water, the people in the church are shouting and praising God and hollering to high heaven. The congregation is in some kind of holy Pentecostal trance. I climb out of the tank to these stairs leading to the back room. I run soaking wet to the outhouse — about 20 yards out back — and peed for what felt like forever. Then I kind of mumbled, "Well Lord, I guess I owe you again."

Thinking back on this, I sometimes wish I had just gone ahead and peed in the tank.

When She Sang Amazing Grace

Written by Ray Wylie Hubbard
Snake Farm Publishing (SESAC)

When I was a child my mama would hold me
In her lovin' arms when the storm clouds came along
The darks clouds rising, storms a ragin'
She'd sing an old gospel song
Thunder crashing, lightning flashing
I found comfort in the words that she would sing
Beyond these dark skies there's a rainbow
That only love and the sun'll bring

When she sang "Amazing Grace"
I felt tears in my eyes
When she sang "Circle Be Unbroken"
I knew there were bluer skies

Time rolled on, the circle was broken
Mama went on to somewhere beyond the blue
I started ramblin' that lost highway
Hard livin' took away the child she knew

I started drinkin' and I started gambling
I had no one to look over me
There were no blue skies, only sorrow
I could only hear her sing in my memory

I was runnin' with a wild bunch
Hanging with the rough and the rowdy kind
I was livin' fast and I was dying young
So alone, Lord, I had a worried mind

I was drunk and I was hurtin'
Somewhere on the streets of New Orleans
When I stumbled into a little shelter
I saw an angel with a tambourine

rwh

hey man, ringo is talking about you on his website.
what?
yeah, he's on his website and he's telling how much he likes *snake farm*.
i go to his website and he is.
seems this cat named brent carpenter came to my show at mccabe's in santa monica and bought *snake farm*. he does all ringo's videos and burned him a copy. didn't even buy him one…burned it. can you believe it? i mean he's a big shot tv and film director and editor and he burns it.
anyhow the next time i am playing at mccabe's, brent shows up and ringo and the all starrs are playing at the greek theater the next night and he invites rick richards and me to the gig. close in parking pass too.
we show up and brent takes us backstage and we meet ringo and his beautiful wife barbara, and ringo takes us around and introduces us to all these great musicians and movie stars back there. he's telling them all what a great songwriter i am and that i am really brilliant cause i travel with only a drummer. not a bass player or guitar player but a drummer. he says he loves rick's drums on *snake farm*.
then he says, come out and sing the encore with me on "help from my friends."
rick and i go to the video truck with brent and watch the show.
after an hour and a half, brent says it's time for you to go sing.
i said i thought he was kidding.
he says nope. he's not that nice. he wouldn't have said it if he didn't mean it. (that is the exact quote. verified by brent himself, no lawsuit pending.)
i go up to stage left and ringo comes off and then goes back out and i walk out and i am onstage singing at the greek theater in hollywood california with a fucking beatle.
i just got chills and almost teared up typing this.
so the next time i am in la, brent says ringo wants you to come up to his house.
we go up somewhere in beverly hills.
we are talking and he says he likes my songwriting and especially "stolen horses."
i say i like yours too.

he says nobody really thinks of me as a songwriter… i'm known more for playing drums and being in that band from liverpool.
i say that on *beaucoups of blues* you wrote a song called "coochy coochy" that is a one chord groove-fest
ah yes, kinda forgot about that one.
i love it and might record it.
well if you do, i'd love to hear it.
so about a year later we're in the edith bates old chapel in round top texas recording *grifters hymnal,* and i have a resonator, george reiff the bass player has a 12 string, rick richards the drummer has a bird feeder and a kick drum, and audley freed, the great guitar player from sheryl crow has a mandolin. i say let's do "coochy coochy."
steve christensen rolls the tape and we do. at the beginning as we are getting in the pocket, i make these growling noises.
we send it to ringo.
we're mixing the record at george's house a few weeks later and i get this phone call. i walk outside and it's ringo from england and he says the drums are cool, so i just sang on it, played guitar and shakers and hit a cymbal a couple of times. mix it however you want.
i say well, there's these funky growls and stuff at the beginning we'll take out.
he says to leave 'em in.
i walk into george's kitchen and tell him that ringo is sending us the track back with him on it and he is going to be mixing a beatle.
he says you know on those george martin records they doubled the vocal tracks...i wonder if he did on this.
he did.
to hear ringo's voice come through the speakers in george's funky old house/studio was a moment more thrilling than…than...er…hmm…anything except maybe lucas' and cory's first cries when they were born into the world.
it is in the top three.
so my undying thanks to richard starkey for his generosity and to cheap ass brent carpenter for burning the cd for him.

Stolen Horses

Written by Ray Wylie Hubbard
Snake Farm Publishing (SESAC)

I'll be riding stolen horses when you don't see me no more
I'll be riding stolen horses on some distant shore

Now reincarnation as I understand it is birth, death and rebirth
Unless we get enlightenment, full tilt enlightenment
We come back down here on earth
And I suppose when we leave here, that we go to some celestial realm
And in one of these Heavens there might be horses
And if there is I'm gonna steal me a few of them

I'll be riding stolen horses when you don't see me no more
I'll be riding stolen horses on some distant shore

Now there's little demons on the Hindu temples
Above the door and all around
What that says is we get past what scares us
And we can stand on sacred ground
So don't be crying when I'm done breathing,
The way I'm living, I'll be back again
So close your eyes and see me riding
Some stolen horses in the wind

chapter 2
Party Line

Now growing up in Southeastern Oklahoma in the early '50s was okay. We lived in a little house with an outhouse and a storm cellar out back, next to my grandparents Jack and Tilda Petty who had some chickens and pigs further out back. My dad, Royce, was the principal, basketball coach and a teacher at Soper School, grades one through twelve in an old red brick building. He came back from the army after WW2 and married my mom, Helen, on January 12 of 1946; I fell out November 13 that same year. My other grandparents were Earl and Annie Hubbard. They lived about four miles away on about 30 acres and had a cow, two mules, a tractor, chickens and pigs, and an old crank phone that if you got too close to the mouthpiece, would randomly shock you. It was on what they called a party line.

Sometimes the phone would ring and my grandfather would answer it, "hello...goddam it!"

rwh

so terry ware, clovis robilaine, jim herbst and some girl i met somewhere, were in the van returning from playing at the palomino club in north hollywood. we pulled in to the howard johnson's on the sunset strip. it was summer and the windows were down and as we parked at the back of the hotel, two men walked up on each side of the van and one stuck a gun in my face as i was in the passenger seat, and the other one stuck a pistol in clovis' face as he was driving and said almost at the same time, this is a robbery, motherfucker. give us your wallets.

i said sure, hang on a minute, i got on leather pants.

clovis said, well i'll give you my money but i can't give you my wallet cause it has my driver's license in it and it took me three times to pass my driving test in oklahoma and...

the guy said gimme the wallet.

clovis said no way.

the guy said gimme the wallet

i said give him the wallet

clovis said i can't parallel park worth a shit and have no idea what a yellow triangle sign means and i ain't gonna do it.

the guy said gimme me money then.

clovis opens his wallet and gives him the 20 dollars in it, terry hands him maybe 35, and jimmy pulls out 10 and i hand him probably 50.

the girl said you sorry motherfuckers, if you want my money, come get it.

i said look, here's the money from my wallet, you got jimmy's money, and buffalo's and clovis'. let's call it a good robbery and this girl i really only met her tonight so...

the guys walk off and get about 30 feet away when the girl climbs over me and opens the door and gets out and yells, you dumbass bastards will burn in hell and starts walking toward them. i jump out, grab her and whisper let 'em go. i got the 1200 dollars from the gig in my boot.

she shoots them the double finger as a car pulls up and they get in. we run to see the license plate but it's too late.

we run around the side of the hotel to go in and call

the police when little richard comes walking out the front door and asks, do you have change for a hundred dollar bill?
jimmy says we did, but we just got robbed.
little richard says lawdy miss clawdy.

chapter 3
Oaths

As a kid in Oklahoma, things were pretty okay. I had a dog, a bb gun, chickens, mules, tractors, barns, woods, ponds, worms, fishing poles, cousins, firecrackers, stray cats, a storm cellar, kites, funny grandparents, and a mom and dad who adored me. I had been going to Sunday school consistently now, so I knew the Ten Commandments. When I got my bb gun, my mother told me I was not to shoot at living things. My grandpa Petty convinced her to let me shoot at wasps and dirt dobbers. (This meant you had to get pretty close to a wasp if you wanted to hit it and if you missed you had better be ready to run.)

One summer, I saw a sparrow on a tree limb and even though I knew it was against God's law and my mama's, I shot it. It fell to the ground and was trembling and shaking, and as I stood over it watching it die, I felt this enormous sadness and guilt and horrific feeling that I had shot a part of God himself. I swore I would never kill another thing so long as I lived. Then I buried the small bird. A few days later as I was walking back home I got stung by a wasp, so I renegotiated my oath to exclude spiders, wasps, flies, and snakes.

Now my father would drink a beer or two at family events, but never lost control or got drunk that I remembered until one July afternoon, after playing dominos in Hugo. He drove up in the old Ford coupe and fell out the door. He was in a complete blackout. My mama's eyes filled with tears as she carried him in the house. She got him some coffee, but he had passed out on the kitchen floor. He slept until about nine that evening. My mama and I sat at the table in silence for the duration. He came to, and my mama gave me a fruit jar and said, "Ray, go outside and catch me some fireflies." I went outside, and since it was summer, I came around and listened at the open window.

My dad said "Honey, I'm sor...." My mom interrupted with a soft quite voice and said, "Royce, I love you and I will always love you, but I will not be married to a drunk. If you come home drunk again, I will take this wedding ring you gave me on the day we were married, and I will take it off, and I will not give it back to you or even throw it way. I will take it and I will melt it down into a bullet." He didn't drink for 22 years, until after my mom was killed. She was out walking with my aunt in Oak Cliff, Texas, down the street by the curb, because there were no sidewalks where we lived. A teenager came speeding around a corner doing about 60 and hit her. As the car came around the corner, she pushed my aunt out of the way saving her life by giving up her own. My dad heard the collision and came running out and found her, and was holding her in the ambulance when she died. They took her into the emergency room and left Dad in the waiting room. The doctor came out and declared her dead. When Dad when in to see her, she was lying on the gurney, and someone had stolen her wedding ring.

Bones

Written by Ray Wylie Hubbard
Snake Farm Publishing (SESAC)

When the sun comes up Mama's singing "Ain't No Cane
on the Brazos"
The sun goes down she's moved on to "Rise Up Poor Lazarus"
Daddy comes in in a gabardine suit and says "Go Fire Up the
Rocket"
He throws me the keys to the 88 and slips some dice in his pocket

Shakin' them bones
Shakin' them bones
Shakin' them bones
Ah baby needs a new pair of shoes

We drive out of town across the river to this club called
Three Deuces
We walk in and my daddy says "I'm feeling my juices"
There's a crap game going on in the back room and right off he
throws a seven
He says "Let it ride" and with the devil's good graces the old man
throws an eleven

He throws Little Joe from Kokomo, and a Fever in the Funk House
Eighter from Decatur, and the Preachers in the Whorehouse
Now there ain't no gambling or loud talk on the streets of glory
The losers say roll them dice and the winners tell smutty stories
It seems all the money in the civilized world is bet on his next toss
And he's praying to them gambling gods for a Neener Ross on a
Faughtin Hoss

Now when the sun comes up mama's singing "Fattening Frogs
for Snakes"
Me and Daddy walk in and he says "Hey baby we had
what it takes"
"You also had some loaded dice" mama says and she kisses him
"And I'm just glad I didn't have to get you out of the criminal
judicial system"

so david letterman comes over as we are plugging in and asks do you know guy clark.
yes i do.
he says, i like him.
i do too.
dave starts to walk back to his desk and i say i did a show with guy in nashville about four months ago and he said we were getting at the age where we could hide our own easter eggs. dave laughs and goes back to his desk and sets down and says to the audience i was just talking to ray about guy clark and guy said he and ray were getting to the age where they can hide their own easter eggs. dave told a joke that guy clark told to me.
i'm looking around at my guys setting up getting ready to perform and i realize it's on the same stage that elvis, the beatles and the stones had been on. i had seen them in black and white on the ed sullivan show when i was a kid. about six months prior to this, keith case who is my agent, gets this phone call: this is jennifer from worldwide pants and dave would like ray to play on his show january 9th and perform the song "mother blues." keith says well let me make sure he's not playing a happy hour gig in waco that night. those are really hard to reschedule.
i assume jennifer thought he was kidding as she didn't hang up on him. she says we have three minutes and 35 seconds to do the song. keith calls judy and i hear her scream and she comes in and tells me my ass is gonna be on late night with dave letterman. six months is a long long time to worry about fucking up on national television. i get on the internet and find me a cool mandarin suede jacket made near pakistan and i order it. i may be old but i'm gonna be old with a cool jacket. george reiff and rick richards have been out with joe walsh for a year so i had been using kyle schiender on drums and john michael schoepf on bass when i did band gigs. Even though rick and george played on the record i decide to go with kyle and john as i felt they deserved it, they had been with me for the last year at some funky ass rough gigs. we get together to rehearse the week before to practice cutting out two verses and getting it within the time requirements and lucas says i think i wanna play this in open e tuning. i

say have you ever played in open e? he says no. i say don't ya think this might be little late to learn all that since we gonna be on tv in front of millions of people in five days.

he shrugs his shoulders and tunes his a string up to b, his d string up to e and his g string up to g#. i pack my mandarin coat, my new $100 jeans (maybe be the first pair of jeans i ever spent that much on), these rough out boots with cactus on them, this purple pullover long sleeve shirt, a scarf someone gave me, and this cap kyle let me borrow cause i look better in it than him, and put them in a separate bag than my other regular clothes. judy, lucas, kyle, john and i land in new york and get to the hotel. it is so hectic and i get distracted, so when we get to the hotel i realize i did not get the bag with my stage clothes off the carousel. i get sick to my stomach. i'm doomed. we get a cab and after a 45 minute cab ride get to the airport and the cabbie pulls up in front of this line of other cabs and says i'll wait till the cops run me off. i run in and there it is. i come back out and the cabbie, judy and some cops and other drivers are about to rumble. i yell loud enough for passengers in planes taking off to hear. i got my clothes for letterman...i got my clothes for letterman. they all stop screaming at each other, look at me. i smile and judy and i get in the cab and the driver jumps in and we drive off. for some reason i get this feeling inside like the time my cousin didn't die when i hit him in the head with a rock.

we rehearse the song that afternoon and everyone is great to us. mattson and kim rainier, joshua and kimberley jones and jeremy tepper hang out with judy and the band in the upstairs greenroom. mattson, josh and jeremy are heavyweight hot shot big deal americana radio cats that also happen to be my friends. we play the song "mother blues," and after we finish dave says goodnight, and then he asks us to sing "screw you we're from texas" for the studio audience. lucas retunes his les paul back to standard and we do it and it was kinda weird singing it for an iconic tv guy from indiana and an audience who probably didn't know who the hell i was in the first place, but we rocked. my only regret is i didn't sing the last line of the song as "screw leno, we're on letterman."

Mother Blues

Written by Ray Wylie Hubbard
Snake Farm Publishing (SESAC)
"Polk Salad Annie" reference used courtesy of Tony Joe White and EMI/Combine Music

When I was a young man about 21 years old y'all
All I wanted was a stripper girlfriend and a Gold Top Les Paul
Be careful of the things you wish for, you might get 'em

There was a night club in Dallas, called Mother Blues
It's where Lightning Hopkins played and Freddie King even paid some dues
All the dealers, and gamblers and young white hipsters
They all made the scene
The girl at the door who checked IDs was just 16
It was not a place for law abiding citizens

Jackie Jones had him a habit, he just couldn't stop
Said "Give me 500 dollars and I'll sell you my Les Paul God Top"
I drove my daddy's car down to Ross Avenue and I sold it
I guess I should have told him he eluded to the police someone stole it
It was just the first of many bad decisions I was to make for the next 20 years
Oh but I had me a guitar

Everybody knows that the real nightlife begins after the clubs close
What they call after hours
It's 2 am and everybody's gone but the band, the dealers and Jack Jones
And then the girls from the Landing Strip club come over
After they put their clothes back on
So I'm at Ma Blues and I'm sitting on an amp, I'm playing "Twist and Shout"
And this tall drink of water walks in and she looks like she might have to shoot her way out

She come up to me and she said "You know anything good on that guitar?"
I didn't say nothing, I just kept on playing
She said "Have you ever heard this song called 'Polk Salad Annie?'"
I just kept playing
She said "Every time I hear that song my insides feel like warm butter and I just wanna take off my clothes and dance around in my underwear"

I said "Down in Louisiana, where the alligator grow so mean"
That's all I knew of it and it was enough
So we hit it off me and this dancer
We hit it off like a metaphor
Like a metaphor for a hydrogen bomb

We was enriched uranium, super critical mass, we was a chain reaction
It was love and lust, mostly lust but a mutual attraction
So there I was boys at 21 years old, I had it all
I had a fine stripper girlfriend and a Gold Top Les Paul

The future, it looked promising
Oh but there were dark clouds on the horizon

She was a beautiful girl but she liked to drink Tequila and that ain't all
I come home 4 or 5 times and she'd pawned my Les Paul
We broke up and she went to Hollywood, she married an actor
She got a job dancing on the Hudson Brothers TV show
And modeling lipstick for Max Factor

I got over her, I'm glad she done alright

Well now me, I never busted through the gates into the big time as a rock and roll star
For 40 years I just carried around an old Gold Top guitar
But love and fate are mysterious things in this funky old world

It was 20 years ago I ended up marrying that Mother Blues
door girl
We had us a boy, he's 18 years old now. He's playing guitar
He ended up with that Les Paul Gold Top, yes he did
Now I don't know if he's gonna hang his life on it or not,
But I'm very grateful for the time I get to share the stage
with him
I'm grateful that I get to write these old songs and travel around
the world and play them for people
And they come out and hear me play
And the days that I keep my gratitude higher than my
expectations
Well, I have really good days

Screw You, We're From Texas

Written by Ray Wylie Hubbard
Snake Farm Publishing (SESAC)

I got on my cowboy boots, jeans and Hawaiian shirt, mirrored sunglasses and a mobile phone
I guess I look like some Port Aransas dope dealer that's out on bail just trying to get home
Well I ain't in jail and I got a guitar, got a little band that's hotter than a rocket
Sometimes we're sloppy, we're always loud, tonight we're just ornery and locked in the pocket

So screw you, we're from Texas
So screw you, we're from Texas
So screw you, we're from Texas
We're from Texas baby, so screw you!

Now I love the USA and the other states they're OK
Texas is the place I wanna be and I don't care if I ever go to Delaware anyway
'Cause we got Stubbs, Gruene Hall and Antones, and John T's Country Store
We've got Willie and Jacky Jack, Robert Earl, Billy Joe and so many more.

Now Texas has gotten a bad reputation, cause of what happened in Dallas and Waco
Our corporations, well they are corrupt and our politicians are swindlers and loco
But when it comes to music my friend, these words are as true as St. John the Revelator's
Our Mr. Vaughan was the best there ever was and no band was cooler than the 13th Floor Elevators.

So screw you, we're from Texas
So screw you, we're from Texas
So screw you, we're from Texas
We're from Texas, so screw you!

chapter 4

Testicles, Baptist Sex, Beer

One day when I was eight, my dad came home and said he got a job teaching in Dallas. We moved to Oak Cliff, Texas and I enrolled in John H. Reagan elementary school as a fourth grader. The first day there I learned that overalls and being tow-headed lends itself to being ridiculed quite easily by all the Gene Vincent looking future convicts of the upper grades. I transferred to Rosemont Elementary school where my Dad taught, so I once again I was a target, except this time by well-to-do young crew-cut rich future-get-away-with-it-'cause-of-daddy's-connections, white collar crime, madras-wearing criminals. I remember falling out of a swing and landing on my face and getting in a few fights so the left side of my face seemed to stay swollen throughout the fifth grade. So nothing much special happened during my sixth and seventh grades. I really had no close friends and had to dodge thuggy rich kids on my way home from school. My mom worked at Western Union and my dad didn't get home till six or so. After I rode my bike home, I would get on the bus and ride to the downtown library. I spent every free hour there and knew the Dewey Decimal system forwards and backwards. I read all the Look, Life, Colliers, Boys Life, Popular Mechanics and Popular Science magazines from the 1930's to the then-present late fifties. I got into Twain and Hawthorne and Poe and Hemingway.

When I was going into the eighth grade I took a physical and the doctor said my testicles hadn't dropped and that he could give me hormone shots but he felt it was too late for that and that surgery would be necessary. Talk about fear rising up and exploding in your head. There was going to be these sharp objects around what I considered to be a very precious area. I was terrified. He gave me the shots but was very doubtful and said if the little critters didn't come home to roost that way he would cut me open and push them down. As I remember, those were his words exactly. Time to pray again. At my next appointment they were still up there. The doctor said let's schedule surgery and I teared up and my mom said, "Anything else we can do?"

The doctor said another shot wouldn't work but he would try it anyway, but we should schedule the surgery. I prayed every night that week trying to make deals and figure out what I could trade and bargain with. Finally, before I went to sleep the day I was to go in, I lay in bed and said, "God, no more begging for you to let these things drop. But if they do and I don't have to have surgery, I promise you I will always be good." During the night I felt this warm sensation in my lower belly and beneath my penis. The doctor couldn't believe it. There they were. Right where they were supposed to be. I walked out of his office a happy man even though I was 13 years old. I thanked God from the bottom of my heart as we drove home and swore once again I would be good for the rest of my life.

Now I had done my five years in a row without missing a Sunday and kept my end of the bargain with the Lord to let my cousin Billy live, so I didn't have to go anymore, but I still went to church with my mama. Dad said he would just take his chances with whatever happened in the hereafter. A couple of Sundays after the testicles dropping, I found myself looking at this girl named Shirley who was 15 and in the choir. I had seen her before but now she looked different. She had a reputation as a fast girl. My voice was still cracking and I didn't know the first thing about singing, but I volunteered to join the choir. She pretty much ignored me since I was 13 and she was 15, but for some reason I kept looking at her out of the corner of my eye at practice. One Sunday morning after a few weeks of singing in the choir, while we were sitting in the loft in our robes behind the pulpit, the preacher asked the congregation to bow their heads and pray. I felt Shirley's hand touch my thigh and proceed to move toward my newly fallen balls. I had never felt anything like this before. It was strange and scary and wonderful and obviously the best thing that had ever happened to me. It was a long prayer and when the preacher said "Amen," I opened my eyes and she was looking straight ahead and now I was completely confused. The ninth grade was awful except for Baptist choir practice. For the tenth grade I went to W.H. Adamson High School while all the students I had gone to school with from the fifth to the ninth grade with went to Sunset. So I was the new hillbilly loner kid once again. I took a drafting class and found out after I walked in that this was the class for the underachievers who had failed a couple of times: Full-tilt-Lucky-Strike-smoking-leather-jacket-hot-rod-knife-toting-cussing-underage-beer-drinking, blackboard jungle hoodlums. The teacher was deathly afraid of them. Nobody bothered me because I knew these seniors John and Paul, the two toughest guys in school. I let them cheat off my paper during tests and had an invisible cloud of protection around me from the other bad guys in school. I guess I could explain this period of time best by saying I went into high school with a greasy Gene Vincent, "Be Bop A Lula" haircut, and came out three years later with a British Invasion "Love Me Do" mop top.

The times were indeed a-changing. In the eleventh grade I got my drivers' license and was coming home from somewhere about ten o'clock, when I went by Kip's Big Boy restaurant. I saw a bunch of seniors and my protector Paul. I pulled in, parked and walked over to where they were sitting on the trunk of a car. He asked if I wanted a beer. Without hesitation I said yes. He gave me a Miller High Life. I opened it and the smell was amazing. I took a sip, then a swallow and I belonged: On this earth and with these guys — I fit. I was no longer a hillbilly rube dumb ass. I was James Dean, baby. I drank all of the beer as fast as I could when one of the guys asks Paul if he wants to see his new deer rifle, a thirty aught six bolt action. We walk over to his car and open the trunk and he hands Paul this rifle.

"It's loaded," he said. We are in the parking lot of a restaurant on a busy street in Oak Cliff, Texas, and Paul says, "See that street light across the road about 60 feet away?" He pulls the bolt back and then slides it forward, flips off the safety, raises the gun to his shoulder, aims and fires. I don't know which was louder, the gun firing or the streetlight exploding. For a moment everybody froze, then the guy whose gun it was grabbed it and threw it in the trunk. And then it was cussing and scrambling, and guys jumping in car windows and peeling out, and I got in my car and sped away and looked in the rear view mirror. Everybody was gone and Paul is walking calmly into the restaurant. I stopped at a convenience store, bought some gum, got home, and my folks were already in bed. I laid down and thought about what happened and wondered how I was going to get some more beer.

rwh

newsflash…stop the presses…call tmz…a scoop.
well the truth is that all this could be wrong but it's the way i kinda remember it. if it's not right, i'm sure my old guitar player terry ware, the avenger of truth, will let me know.
so back sometime ago whenever it was, terry talked me into bringing a young keyboard player named dave gant into the band…he was great…hammond b3 and a leslie. it was cool. just a soulful player…grew up on all the motown and memphis stuff. his dream was to play in a funk and soul band.
well things kinda fell apart as they do with bands.
we still kept in touch.
so he calls me one day and says he has an opportunity to go to vegas and play in a big name casino show band with horns and dancers and where he'll have his own tech and the money is just jaw dropping great or…he has a chance to do some demos somewhere in oklahoma with just another one of these young wannabe dime a dozen country singers nobody has ever heard of.
i said dave, forget the kid. go to vegas, man. that okie dufus will never amount to a hill of beans.
after playing with me for a while and knowing my good judgment in all things that have to do with the music business…he said, nah. i think i'll go record these demos with this kid named garth brooks.
last time i ran into him in nashville he didn't gloat but he did let me know very subtly that he had gotten a new lexus every two years since that conversation.
any of you guys want some show business advice?

chapter 5

"Benevides Los Coachmen"

Now I had an old Silvertone guitar that I could play the *Peter Gunn* theme on it (you know, duh da duh da duh da duh da) but it was cheap and hard to play and wouldn't stay in tune. There was this cheerleader named Michael Murphey who performed in this folk group called the Kingsmen at an assembly one day. Not the "Louie, Louie" Kingsmen. They just had the same name.

He was the most popular guy in school. Even the thugs liked him.

I went home and got that guitar and learned "Tom Dooley."

There was this cool guy in my class named Rick Fowler. He was a member of the Key Club and seemed to be a smart ass. I sat next to him in some class and overheard him say he had a guitar. I said I had one too. He didn't seem that impressed. For some reason he invited me over to his house one afternoon and he had this Harmony Sovereign and picked it up and was great. He could fingerpick "Freight Train" and "Aw Babe Ain't No Lie." I said "Will you teach me how to do that?" He said, "No."

But I had seen the light. He loaned me a couple of records, one being the Kingston Trio. I kept going over to his house and we began to learn some of their songs and he said he knew another guy who played and sang named Wayne Kidd. We hung out that summer and learned, "I Know You Rider, Delia's Gone," and of course, "Greenback Dollar."

So now I was in a folk trio and drove the family car, a 1964 Ford Fairlane, and I'd had some experience with girls. Well, one anyway. I was now taking Shirley home after Sunday night service and had completely forgotten the covenant I made with God to be good after my testicles dropped. What we were doing would be tame today, but then it was low down and dirty and fun.

So our first gig is playing for Wayne's little sister's eighth grade Spanish class banquet at El Fenix restaurant in Oak Cliff. Rick's mom buys us matching short sleeve striped shirts and we are big time. We show up and they have a podium with a gooseneck mike on it for the P.A. system. There's no room for our instruments so we leave them in the kitchen. There's about 16 kids and the teacher, and it is required for all the students to speak Spanish. It's freezing in the place and we're sitting at the table not knowing what anybody's saying, and eating sherbet for desert after the meal. Suddenly, the teacher gets up and walks to the podium and says, "Por favor Benevides Los Coachmen." Then he sits down.

We realize that this is our introduction. We go into the kitchen get our guitars and Rick's banjo, and bring them into the ice-cold dining room. We go up to the podium and I look at Wayne and he has checked out. He looks scared. He starts strumming the chord for "Rider," and I notice that his capo is on the wrong fret. I look at Rick and he is now changing the capo on his banjo, which means he has to turn the high g string to the right pitch. The change in temperature has caused everything to go out of tune. The song is now higher than we rehearsed it and after the ice cream and the fact that we are shivering, our vocals crack and we can't hit the notes. It is the Titanic sinking. We finish the song with this three-part harmony screech and there is no applause, just the look of horror on these eighth grader's faces.

We have one joke rehearsed. Wayne is to say, "For those of you who know this song, it's called 'Delia's Gone.' For those of you who don't, it's still called 'Delia's Gone.'" Instead Wayne says, "For those of you who know this song, it's called 'Delia's Gone,' and for those that don't know it, we don't care."

Wayne is now completely gone. I am in no better shape, my hand is shaking as I take off my capo and Rick just looks disgusted.

I now have no idea where I am. I just want to go home. I glance at Wayne's sister and it appears she has tears in her eyes.

After we finish singing "Delia's Gone," Rick has the stamina to say "thank you, good night," saving us the terror and embarrassment of attempting another song.

The teacher hands Wayne an envelope as we go into the kitchen to get our cases. It has 15 dollars in it.

rwh

i'm driving somewhere and my cell phone rings.
hey ray, its ronnie dunn.
who?
ronnie dunn.
who?
ronnie dunn. of brooks and dunn.
who the hell is this?
it's ronnie dunn. of brooks and dunn.
are you the one in the hat?
no, i'm the other one. tony joe white gave me your number.
at that point i realize it's really ronnie dunn.
oh, ronnie dunn...sorry 'bout the hat remark. i thought it was one of my buddies jacking with me.
he says he told tony joe he liked my *grifters* album and tony said we should get together and write so he was calling to see if we could set it up.
so we did.
now ronnie dunn is a huge country star but you may not be aware that he is also one badass full tilt walking cool songwritin' son of a bitch.
we wrote five songs together. he came to austin and i got rick richards and george reiff who had been out with joe walsh for a year, brad rice on guitar from son volt and ian mclagan from the small faces to record with him…it was stonesy early black crowesy dirty lowdown most pure evil bumping and grinding cool as hell roots rock pentecostal backseat sex nasty.
i hope someday that project is released.

South of the River

Written by Ray Wylie Hubbard
Snake Farm Publishing (SESAC)

Wake that thing up and put some clothes around it
You've lost your prescription, I found it
You need some good rocking, nothing painful
Like my friends, The Heathens and Black Angels

It's a good night for rocking, south of the river
It's a good night for rocking with a band that delivers
It's a good night for rocking, deep in the south
It s a good night for rocking, putting something in your mouth

Aw, child you should have heard the *James Gang Rides Again*
It was like shooting salvation and funk into your soul back then
There's some homicidal young bands that still rock like that
They'll cut your throat with bass, drums, Les Pauls and Strats

Wake that thing up and make sure it's still bleeding
The tubes are warmed up, now I got what you're needing
Now there's some risk seeing we're dressed like thieves
We are among the righteous, the ones who believe

chapter 6
Warm Beer

For some reason known only to God, after our debut at the Pan-American banquet, the Coachmen didn't break up. We played some assemblies that fall. Rick, of course, was the main attraction to the girls, and Wayne was a serious smart guy, and I was...I don't know what, but I was known in school. I couldn't sing harmony or play that good, but I did like the idea of folk music and what it stood for.

Rick gave me a Bob Dylan album 'cause his parents thought it was awful and didn't want it in the house. I took it home and loved it. I then found Woody Guthrie and Leadbelly and Jimmy Rodgers and Cisco Houston. I was now a folkie; I got me some desert boots and a work shirt.

My folks were going up to Hugo, Oklahoma to check on my grandma every weekend; she was in a nursing home. My other grandparents had died during the past couple of years. My parents left about four o'clock one Friday afternoon; I got an older guy to get me a case of Miller.

By seven o'clock I was right. I was drinking by myself and really liked it, just getting kind of fuzzy and stumbling around. I guess this means that from the very beginning I was never a social drinker. I wasn't drinking socially, I was just drinking. I was putting the empties in a trashcan four houses down the alley and hid the rest of the beer in the garage and laid down with the world spinning round and sure liked the way it made me feel.

I woke up about ten the next morning and didn't feel too bad. I had it figured out: I could drink that day and night and be okay by Sunday afternoon when my folks got home. So I went out in the garage and got a church key and opened a warm beer and drank it.

rwh

okay this is going to be a whore dog gig. i want you to know it up front. i would advise you not to take it if you if you have any misgivings at all. its called the texas redneck games and it is in east texas and it will be crappy but the money is really good and it's one 75 minute set and its 2500 dollars and i told them they could not advertise your name in dallas and we could really use the money and you could pay whoever you wanted to play it with you like 300 a man and after expenses and commissions we would net a grand, twelve hundred bucks, and we kinda need the money and no one in austin would find out and it will be just play, take the money and run and how bad could it really be? i mean after all you wrote "redneck mother" so you kind of started this celebration of lowlife white trash motherfuckers anyway, so whadyathink?

judy waited for my answer knowing i would say yes but giving me a chance to say no. i say yeah, how bad could it really be? i mean after all, just rick and i opened for david allan coe at this club called gators in gun barrel city, texas, and the opening band before us was a lynyrd skynrd, guns 'n' roses tribute band and that went pretty well.

i pick up george reiff and scrappy jud newcomb and darren hess and as we are driving up toward kilgore we see a falling down dumpy red building with a yellow sign on wheels out front that says 'band tonight,' and i say at least we're not playing there. little did i know in less than six months i would be.

we get to the site of the 'games' about nine o'clock and it is like a 1930 oklahoma dust storm. from the earth to the sky there is this horrible brown hazy cloud blocking out the full moon that is created from every off road vehicle sold in the south since 1980 roaring all over this giant dirt field with texas and rebel flags flying from the handlebars and there are more locusts swarming in the air than there ever were because of yahweh's curse upon pharaoh in the book of *exodus*. i am getting sick to my stomach. we pull up backstage and the band opening for us is playing "friends in low places" and throwing condoms with their logo on them to the crowd. the promoter comes up and tells us the redneck comedian from nashville got too drunk to perform but crawled on stage during the wet t shirt contest and started fondling the girls and got a microphone and started making comments so rude even the drunk rednecks in the crowd were offended and threatened to beat the shit out of him. the promoter had to hold a fifth of bourbon in front of him to get him offstage and into a pickup truck to take him to the hotel.

as george and i walk down toward the midway looking for the food tents we hear the emcee announce that there is a tie in the butt crack contest. i have lost my appetite. as we are waiting in line at some sausage stand, the guy in front of us who has no shirt on is talking to a twenty something redneck girl and she asked him about the chinese symbol that is tattooed on his neck. he says and this is a direct quote: that's my name in oriental. she says, cool. as we walk away george says he always wondered what the chinese symbol was for "bubba." i recognize the taste of bile in my throat. we have backed the van up to the ramp on the left side of the stage and are waiting to unload and set up. i am in the driver's seat looking into this dirt field with the stage and audience behind me. scrappy, george and darren have walked over a few car lengths and are watching the band play "you don't have to call me darlin', darlin." i see some movement in this pasture about 30 feet in front of the van and i think it is a cow or goat or something. i squint to see what it is.

i figure it out and roll down the window and say, hey, scrappy. he and george and darren turn around and i turn on the headlights and illuminated through the haze is a 40 year old ugly male Texas redneck game patron wearing a straw cowboy hat with his camouflage pants wadded up down around his work boots and an even uglier 40 year old Texas redneck game woman patron with her cutoff jeans in her left hand and they are fucking each other standing up in the middle of this field among 10 or so cows. they don't stop or even slow down when the lights hit them. i turn the headlights off after a minute or so and lay my head on the steering wheel and think to myself that the first of the seven seals has been broken and i soon will hear the sound of hoof beats. we get on stage and i say the hell with it and the first song i play is redneck mother. the crowd is rabid. we are like the greatest thing these human-like people have ever seen. it is as if we are playing for some caligula roman orgy or a new year's eve party in sodom or gomorrah. women are bumping and grinding against each other as men in camouflage drool and clap their hands and throw back their heads and howl like dogs seeing a full moon for the first time. in front of scrappy two twenty something girls are making out in the crowd. george is watching barrel chested men chug beer then crush the cans on their forehead. darren is keeping time while a forty year old woman from the side of the stage keeps flashing her breasts at him. my nose is caked with dust and my throat is sore and raw and there are locusts in my hair but any shame or embarrassment i have has taken a back seat to the abandoned frenzy and deranged adoration I am receiving from the redneck gamers.

we are rock and roll. we are decadent. we are golden. after every song i shout, is anyone drunk yet? The roar from the crowd is deafening. now scrappy has played with ian maclagan and ron wood has set in with him. george has done gigs with chris robinson, jakob dylan, the dixie chicks and joe walsh. darren hess has played with green on red, james mcmurtry and bruce robison…all three have done the late night tv shows and rock festivals and toured europe and japan. yet each will tell you that the east texas redneck games they played with me for 300 dollars one dusty, bug filled night near tyler, is their favorite gig of all time.

chapter 7

Red River, Mance, $12.50 a night

In the spring of our senior year, Rick came up to me with a flyer. He said, "Look at this."

It was something he got off the bulletin board at school: *Looking For Talented High School Graduates to Perform at a Resort in New Mexico.* "We should audition for this."

The man who put up the poster was T.A. Painter. We went over to his house and auditioned. The next day he called and told us we got the gig but we had to get approval from our parents. So we all went over to his house again with our folks and found out the details: 500 dollars a month to perform each night — except Wednesday — for June, July and August in Red River, New Mexico. Our folks agreed with the stipulation we called them once a week.

I was just ready to split, daddy-o. So ready, I did not go the senior prom, and don't even remember going to graduation, being in a robe or getting my diploma. I guess I did, but I don't remember it.

We got on a bus in downtown Dallas with three guitars, a banjo and three trunks. Off we went on a 28-hour Trailways bus trip to Questa, NM. At one point after 18 hours or so, we got the whole bus to sing, "Help Me, Rhonda." Painter picked us up in the rain and drizzle, and we drove 13 miles to Red River and pulled up to the ski chalet; it looked cool. Then we found out that the place we're staying in is around back. It's a cinder block storage room with three cots; the bathroom is on the other side of some stairs by the trash cans.

We unloaded our stuff and Painter said, "Boys, there's some other duties required." We spent the next six hours sweeping, mopping, wrapping potatoes in tin foil, washing plates, silverware and glasses, slicing tomatoes and onions, making spice cake, and setting up for the BBQ dinner that was to be served the next night. He was having a dinner for the whole town and we were to perform so local motels and such could recommend us to their clients. We have a 40-minute set down pat and when he says we are to perform *three* 45-minute sets each night...panic was too mild a word to describe our situation.

Rick says here's what we do: "We'll each do a song solo for each set; that should lengthen it." The only songs I know by myself are "Old Shep," and "Rake and Ramblin' Boy."

Opening night the place is packed and we did three songs when Rick says: "Here's Ray to do a song for you" then he whispers to me, "kill some time." I asked, "How?" He replied, "Tell 'em about your Okie hillbilly dumbass self."

Now I had never been the talker between songs. Rick was the guy who knew how to introduce songs, and Wayne had perfected his patter of "For those of you who know this song..."

I went up to the microphone and there are about 200 people who don't really seem to care staring at me. They just want their free BBQ and then to get the hell out. I stand there for what seems an eternity and can hear people shuffling uncomfortably in their seats and look at Rick and Wayne off to the side of the stage and Rick says "Say something!"

I finally open my mouth and what comes out is, "My grandmother was a fortune teller and my grandfather was a bootlegger in Oklahoma...he smuggled books into to Arkansas.' I paused for a moment, and then sang "Old Shep."

We got through our sets, but then it was time to mop, wash dishes, stack chairs. We fell exhausted into our cots in our concrete bunker. Wayne went outside and around the building to the bathroom, when we heard a noise out there we looked out the door and a full-grown black bear is digging through the trash about 20 feet away. We hollered through the walls for Wayne to stay put. The bear left about 20 minutes later, and Wayne came running in. It was then that we noticed there was no lock on the door.

We got up the next day and wrapped potatoes and carried Cokes and buns and hot dogs to the chair lift to take to the top of the mountain, where we were required to work in the Treeline Café during the day. Then we had to come down in late afternoon and set the tables for the dinner and show that night, and then do it again every day except Wednesday for the next three months.

After that summer was over, Rick went to Texas Tech, Wayne to Tyler Junior College and I went to Arlington State College. I went to a physics class and decided to change my major to English. I found the bohemian-beatnik-left-intellectual-folk-music people, and just kind of floundered around that year.

By that time the Beatles had made our scene, but Bob Dylan's "Like A Rolling Stone" came along and confused the folkies. I was hanging out at the little folk club in Dallas called The Rubaiyat. The only really interesting thing that I remember, was this great ragtime blues guitar player named Johnny Vandiver came up to me on campus one day and asked if I wanted to go to Oklahoma City that coming Saturday and see Mance Lipscomb perform at a club called The Sword and Stone. I said yes. He asked if I had a car. I told him a '64 Ford Fairlane. Satisfied, he informed me that we'll leave about ten the next morning. I asked him why we had to leave so early, Oklahoma was only four hours away.

He said, "We got to go to Navasota and pick up Mance and take him to the gig."

Johnny was the opener for Mance and was one of the best and most powerful solo performers I have ever seen. Johnny and I stayed at the club owner's house with Mance. After the club closed, we all went over to one of Mances's cousins or aunts or one of his relative's houses and drank homemade chalk beer and played and sang till almost dawn. The beer actually tasted like chalk. When I listen to Mance or Johnny today, I am reminded of that night in OKC and am aware of what a powerful precious moment in time that was.

Sometime that year I started a jug band with Larry Groce playing mandolin, Jerry Graves on washtub bass and this wonderful girl singer Jo Wright on washboard and kazoo. We got a gig at the Rubaiyat in Dallas. Ron Shipman the owner gave us a weekly gig there doing two sets a night paying us $250 dollars a week for the band to split. That's $50 a night split four ways which is $12.50 for each member. We start killing it. We were packing the place on weekends and weeknights were pretty full too. We were the darlings of Dallas folk music ah-fish-ee-ah-nah-doughs. Larry said we should be making more money since we got standing room only crowds. So he went to up Ron and said we'd like to get a $50 raise to $300 a week: which means each band guy would get an extra $2.50 a night.

Ron said, ''Forget it. No way. You're fired.''

Larry went on to host Mountain Stage on NPR, Jerry became a fireman in Lewisville, Texas and I don't know what happened to Jo, but she was my favorite washboard playing hot soul shouting mama ever.

Portales

Written by Ray Wylie Hubbard
Snake Farm Publishing (SESAC)

North of Portales above the cap rock plain
I was lookin' out a window wishing for rain
I found her sleeping in a haystack
I left her dreaming, never been back

It's a hand woven love song of sadness
It's all I sing when I think of you
Morning love sighs, good-byes and madness
Is all I ever gave to you

She was a woman she was barely twenty-five
So nice to look at, wild and alive
She was in love, you know, but I could not see
When she'd say her prayers, she'd say one for me

Sometime that winter I heard that old road
The high wild wind cold and alone
Then she gave me an old ring for my hand
She said, "I know you're leaving, love me while you can"

It's a hand woven love song of sadness
It's all I sing when I think of you
Morning love sighs, good-byes and madness
Is all I ever gave to you

rwh

so david w. and i left kansas with $10,000 in cash, a couple of 8 balls, a case of beer iced down, a bottle of jts brown whiskey and a couple of guns...the future looked promising…it wasn't. about 3 years later i ended up in some rooms with some drunks who weren't drinking talking about not drinking.

what caused this scenario was that bugs henderson and i had played up in kansas at some blues bar and were friends with the biggest dope dealer in the tri-state area.

me and this guy stayed up all night and as the sun was coming up he said he would love just to smoke a joint with willie…i said well if i had the money i could probably record at pedernales studios that willie owned and he could come down and hang out and there was a good chance that might happen. he asked how much would something like that cost…i said we could record an album for 10k. he said cool.

i called willie and said I'd like to record at your studio and how much would he charge me…he said i could have it free for 10 days if i would pay the engineers 5 grand to split. i said cool.

we booked it and went out there to record.

we were there a few days and one night we were recording this song i wrote called "these eyes"… darrell royal walked in the studio and sat down and listened…we finished tracking it and he said willie would really sound good singing on that.

i said well i can't ask him cause he was so nice to give me the studio for nothing. darrell said i'll ask him. he's coming down in a little while to play chess.

so it's about one o'clock in the morning and willie walks in and darrell says willie you should sing on this song ray wrote…willie smiles and says he can't afford me.

darrell says how bout we shoot a game of pool and if i win, you sing for nothing.

willie says okay but if i win, ray pays me what i made off the duet i did with julio iglesias.

i am beginning to feel uncomfortable.

it was decided that gary macdonald who was my bus driver and darrell royal are partners against willie and bobby arnold.

they rack 'em and shoot best 2 out of 3. willie and

bobby win the first game and darrell and gary win the second…it comes down to that bobby only has to sink the 8 ball and they win…he scratched…willie says let's sing the son of a bitch.
the boys from kansas who had been staying in one of the condos walk in about that time and say, willie, we got some weed here that's known as arkansas permafuck...it will permanently fuck you up. they go outside for a while, and then willie goes in the sound booth and sings the song...if you ever hear it, just know he sang it about four in the morning and maybe you can hear the weed...it was thrilling to hear him sing a song i wrote.
i couldn't get it together to put it out on a record so i carried the tape around for about 6 years till cds came in and i put it on *lost train of thought.*
oh yeah, on our last day of recording, david anderson and willie and two men dressed in suits walked through the studio when we were recording. they all went out the door to the foyer…a few minutes later, willie came in and said, when you leave today, take your masters with you.
we finished up and loaded the gear and the tapes and left about midnight.
the next day the IRS locked down the studio.

These Eyes

Written by Ray Wylie Hubbard
Snake Farm Publishing (SESAC)

A woman's heart is such a fragile thing
And love can be so cruel sometimes
So if your heart aches in the long lonely night

Come share your loneliness with mine

I won't do you no wrong
I never will lie
Can't you tell that I love you
By looking in these eyes

When a woman loves a man so strong
The world's a flower every spring
When a man does a woman wrong
The ashes of a rose is all that remains

chapter 8

Texas Twosome, A Fine Proposition

Our folk trio had met some people in Red River who ran Frye's Old Town Souvenir Shop. That April, Wayne told Rick and I that he got a job with them for the coming summer. Somehow the two of us convinced our parents to let us load up the Ford Fairlane and go to up to Colorado, to just bum around and see if we could sing for our supper, a place to stay and tips. (I didn't have a backseat in the car. I believe it was Wayne who, sometime the previous year, threw a cigarette out the window and it came back in and burned it up.)

In June we headed out as freewheeling troubadours and pulled into Red River as a stopover before going to Colorado. We walked into Jack's Riverview Café and Motel and asked for the owner when this funky old man with one weird eye walked up, wiping his hands on a cook's apron and said, "What the hell do you want?"

Rick laid it out: "We're the Texas Twosome and how 'bout we do some singing for these good people eating in your fine establishment and you feed us and put us up for a couple of nights."

He answered, "Why not?"

We commenced pulling out the banjo and guitar. Since there was no stage, we walked right up to these people at their tables while they were eating, like some demented hillbilly version of a violin player at a romantic French restaurant. We started singing "West Texas Highway," and about halfway through the song Jack, the owner/cook, comes out of the kitchen with a washtub bass and starts playing along with us. After the songs finished, he went into this Andy Griffith "What it was, was football," routine.

We went to another table and sang "Greenback Dollar." After we finished, Jack became Bill Cosby and starts doing "Fat Albert." We had become a trio with a front man.

After the café closed, we sat down at a table and Jack brought us out two hamburgers, onion rings, and even though we ordered ice tea, he brought us two Cokes. Then he went back into the kitchen and returned with a fifth of Evan Williams bourbon whiskey and poured some into each of our glasses and stirred it with his finger.

He lit a cigarette and said, "Boys, I got a proposition for you. I got a room behind the washateria across the street you can stay in. Don Dossett's Jeep Tours needs a driver and the Jaycees' information booth is looking for someone to man it. You can trade off days working at those places. And they always need a gunfighter down at the Frye's Old Town Shootout in the afternoon, and you can sing at my place at night."

Then he started doing Jonathan Winters' "Maude Fricker" and adds, "Now boys, there's a lot of horny 19- and-20-year-old Texas and Oklahoma big breasted farm girl tourists that come up here and just love jeep-driving-tour-guide-Jaycee-information-giving-local-gunfightin'-long-haired-folksingers. How about it?"

I answered, "Let's have another drink and we'll think it over."

Rick said, "Exactly how big are these breasts we're talking about?"

We headed off to Colorado the next morning since the Jaycee information booth wouldn't be open for a week. Rick and I decided to seek adventure in the Rocky Mountains. We find this little folk club in Denver and do a guest set as "Jefferson Cross and Austin Graynes." We did our set and slept on the stage that night.

The next night was Sunday and when no one had showed up by around 10 p.m. the waitress went back to the kitchen and Rick and I pulled out our sleeping bags, laid them out on the stage, crawled in them, passed a half pint of Evan Williams back and forth and drifted off to sleep. We awoke from being shaken by the waitress who said three people came in and ordered coffee. We crawled out of our sleeping bags, tuned up and did our set. We spent the next week just driving around Colorado and going into towns and playing and meeting people and just enjoying the experience. We were ramblin' around like Woody Guthrie, freewheelin' like Bob Dylan; just drifting along like tumblin' tumbleweeds.

We cruised back into Red River and moved what stuff we had into the back room of the washateria, which consisted of two cots and a lamp.

Rick and I swapped shifts daily and my routine went like this: Monday, Wednesday, Friday: Jaycee information booth from nine to three, then over to the gunfights where I put on an old cowboy hat and strapped on a six gun with blanks and become Silly the Kid and along with Texas Red and Black Jack Ketchup rob the false front bank, forget to take the money, and then have a shootout where I get hit and fall off the roof. Then I'd clean up and head over to the café and go table to table with Rick singing our songs, as Jack thumped his washtub bass and did his Catskill Mountain comedy routines. After closing, we'd eat burgers and drink Evan Williams with Coke, and stay up and play guitars and laugh 'til we went to cot.

Tuesday, Thursday, Saturday: I would put on a beat up Stetson hat and rough out boots and drive tourists and fishermen up to the old mines and lakes in a long 4-wheel drive C-7 jeep and make up answers for whatever questions they would ask. I'd get back about four, wash the jeep, clean up, then hit the café, sing and eat whatever Jack's wife Edna cooked for us, have a couple of beers — or a Coke with a shot of Evan Williams whiskey in it — then walk across the street to a small knotty pine room, lay down, and drift off to sleep to the sounds of the night people drying their clothes.

rwh

there was this one time in france...
rick richards and lucas and i are over there to play the rendezvous festival.
we are in the lobby of the hotel there in france and lucky tubb who's playing the festival comes in and is upset. seems his cds back in the states didn't get pressed in time so they weren't shipped and he doesn't have any to sell and was hoping to sell enough to pay expenses for the rest of his tour.
he had given me his one advance copy at dinner the night before because he thought they would be there that next morning.
he was distraught.
after a few minutes lucas said, we have a computer. why not go get some blank cds and we could burn some, you know, like one at a time and at least probably maybe get 50 by gig time.
great idea, says lucky, and he's off to find a french version of radio shack.
rick says, that's too bad he didn't get his cds…wonder how he got his nickname.
anyhow we burn a bunch one at a time that night in our room and then the next day head out to the gig and get backstage and there's about 15 people in this little tent…some drinking beer, some wine, some evian, eating snacks…you know, just backstage greenroom stuff. anyhow a little assembly line is set up.
lucas (1) burns a cd on the computer, hands it to another member of lucky's band (2) who puts it in a case and hands it to another band member (3). lucky (4), who has a pair of scissors, cuts out the cover he had printed up to fit the case (two covers to a sheet) and then hands the cut out cover to band member (3) who puts it in the jewel case and closes it.
this process repeats itself over and over and over and over…1 to 2 to 3. 4 to 3. 1 to 2 to 3. 4 to 3. 1 to 2 to 3. 4 to 3…you get the picture..
after about 25, 30 minutes of this, conversation has stopped and it's just the sound of the computer burning the cd, scissors cutting paper and the click of plastic cd jewel cases being snapped shut.
after about 10 minutes of no talking, just these repetitious sounds, lucky says, lucas how old are you?
lucas says seventeen.

there was silence once again with just the sound of the computer, scissors and jewel case snapping shut and then one of the fifteen people in the room who was standing by the tent flap door and who shall remain nameless says, wow. seventeen and playing lead guitar for your father at a huge festival in france...how cool is that? when i was seventeen i was busted for selling 225 pounds of pot to an undercover narcotics agent.
the little assembly line continued in silence for a while and then lucky had to go play.
the audience loved him and he sold all of his cds which i think numbered about 150.
and if lucas ever wants to go to a lucky tubb show, he is on the permanent guest list.

chapter 9

Lottery #127, A Redneck Mother

Somewhere during this period of time, the war in Vietnam was going on. The draft lottery happens and I get number 127. This means that unless I take 12 required hours of college courses I would be drafted. My father — who fought with the 45th Infantry Division at Anzio and Monte Casino, landed in France during Operation Dragoon and continued on into Germany — said I was not to get into this war and both he and my mother would move to Canada with me if it came to that. He said to get out however I could. I think it had to do with Eisenhower's speech of fearing the military industrial complex.

I was not on scholastic probation but I was close. Rick and Wayne's numbers were lower than mine and they even talked about going into the National Guard so they wouldn't end up getting shot at in Southeast Asia. So come that spring I lacked nine hours to receive a degree in English, which meant I would get drafted. Well I just decided to quit going to class altogether and wait it out. I was running with some poet radical types now and the day before I go to my draft physical we stayed up all night drinking wine and singing Woody Guthrie songs and even though I had tried pot a few times and I didn't particularly care for it, I smoked the shit out of that shit that night.

A professor and his artist wife and two other drunk and high antiwar intellectuals dropped me off at the draft board testing center at eight a.m. and one of them gave me a purple pill. I took it with a swallow of warm wine and walked in.

I took some vision and hearing tests and some other stuff. At about 11 a.m. some doctor called my name and he told me to come back in six months. I came out of the building and colors were really bright and swirling around and I was Dorothy in Oz wandering around downtown Dallas for a few hours. I don't remember how I got home but my folks were happy.

The next day when colors had stabilized once again, I told my dad I felt some guilt about dodging the draft. My fathered looked at me and said, "If North Vietnam ever invades California you can volunteer to be a sniper at Disneyland."

So the next summer it was back to Red River as Rick and Wayne didn't join the National Guard and didn't get drafted. Then the conflict ended and the lottery was no longer.

There were three bars in town: the D Bar D which was known as the hardcore-cowboy-redneck-right-wing-pro-war-anti-hippie bar, Tony's, which was about the same, and the Red Onion at the Village Inn Motel where a long-haired musician could buy beer.

One night we were playing songs and drinking beer at our cabin with some of the jeep drivers and other hangers on, just passing the old guitar around. We were low on beer and I got picked to go get a case or two. I took up a collection. The D Bar D was across the street and the Red Onion was at the other end of town, and for some reason, even though no long hair had ever gone into the D Bar D because everybody said it was dangerous, I figured how bad could it really be?

I crossed the street and walked in. I found out.

There were about 15 or 20 rough looking men and one tough old woman sitting at the bar. I walked up to the only space left: Next to the woman and the waitress station. I looked at the bartender square on.

"I need two cases of Miller High Life."

"You got an ID?"

I handed him my driver's license. He took it and looked at it for a long time. The song on the jukebox ended. Another didn't follow it. Nobody said a word. I became the center of attention. It may be a cliché, but the silence was deafening.

The old woman looked at me.

She said: "How can you call yourself an American with hair like that?"

"I don't remember calling myself an American. I just remember asking for a case of beer. "

"My youngest son is in Vietnam."

"You must be proud, I have friends from high school over there and…"

"My other son is standing next to you and we both don't like hippies."

I looked next to me and there was one terrifying dove-and-deer-hunting-ex-convict-True-Grit-John-Wayne-tall-redneck-30-to-35-year-old bad boy, smiling at me with Skoal tobacco teeth. Next to him are two really big 40 year-old men who were looking at me like I was a plague.

"Mama, you want me to kick the shit out of this hippie for you?"

"Go on and kick his hippie ass," someone else said.

"Technically, I'm a musician rather than a hippie," I said trying to be funny, then quickly realized that for humor to work, you've got to have a sense of humor which apparently no one in the D Bar D had.

Dead silence.

The redneck son finished his drink and set the empty glass on the bar.

"Maybe you should sing the "Star Spangled Banner" while I twist your balls off," he suggested.

"Look, I work for Don Dossett over across the street at Jeep Trailways and I also work down at the outpost and…"

The bartender came back with two cases of Miller. I took twenty dollars out of my pocket and laid it on the bar.

"Keep the change."

I picked up the cases and stepped right to go around the woman's son. He stepped left blocking me.

"Not so fast, shithead."

I am doomed.

My last resort?

"Where you all from?"

"Oklahoma."

I said, "I was born in Hugo."

"Well that ain't gonna save you from gettin' your ass stomped."

I looked around and there wasn't sympathy or a friendly face to be found. I had really fucked up.

(God, if you get me out of this, I promise I'll tell everybody what a good God you are...)

The son of the redneck mother looks at me like a hungry jackal that came upon a baby rabbit with its hind leg caught in barbed wired.

I realized I couldn't talk. Nobody was saying anything.

The silence became louder. It was causing a ringing in my ears. I then realize it's this buzzing, humming sound from a neon Coors sign in the front window. It's the only sound. The bartender reached into his back pocket, pulled out a blackjack and looked at the redneck mother's son.

"I don't care if you beat the shit out of him or not. You just can't do it in here."

They stared at each other and the two guys next to her son sat their drinks on the bar and put their cigarettes out in an ashtray and it appeared as if all hell were about to break loose. I wondered if it would do any good to request if they wouldn't mind, not to hit me in face or kick me in the nuts.

I realized that the jukebox had not played a song since I walked in and it came to mind that if Merle Haggard's "Fighting Side of Me," came on, I would never see my family again.

After what seemed like an eternity, a voice said, "Leave the hippie be." It was the old woman's.

The bartender put the blackjack in his pocket. He said, "Son, take your beer and leave."

I walked out, down the stars and across the parking lot.

When I got to the street I glanced back and there was a pickup truck with Oklahoma plates, a gun rack and two bumper stickers. One read, "America - Love It Or Leave It," while the other was, "Goat Ropers Need Love Too."

I got back to the cabin, everybody was singing and I put the beer in the ice chest. The song ended.

"I hope you sons of bitches appreciate what I went through to get this beer. I almost got my ass kicked."

Either B.W. Stevenson or Bob Livingston handed me a guitar — I don't remember which.

I hit a G chord and sang, "He was born in Oklahoma..."

There you go: the real story of the song that refuses to die.

we interrupt your reading for an important announcement: both gibson and martin have artist-endorsed models like the dwight yoakam or kris kristofferson or eric clapton or roy smeck or nick lucas…a whole bunch of 'em. i mean even the guy from staind has got one. sooooo…the ray wylie hubbard model. either a 1949 gibson j45 neck on a 1959 southern jumbo body or a 1951 j45 neck on a 1962 country western body with scars on 'em put there before i got them as i would never treat them like that and with dearmond toaster top pickups mounted behind the sound hole and knobs that tony nobles had laying around in junk parts boxes and pick guards moved so they are not covering the rings and are the most beautiful guitars in the world in my opinion and able to make both little demons and fallen angels dance the hully gully and they play like butter and when heard causes even the most calloused ears to smile and…and…sorry…i lost it there…i guess you get the idea that these two axes of mine are precious to me…even more so than the ring sauron wanted. maybe not monetary wise…i paid 100 bucks for one neck and 150 for the other one and 800 bucks for the country and western and 1200 for the southern jumbo and 125 for each dearmond pickup and paid tony 250 each time to put the necks on 'em but i would not sell them if someone offered me 10,000 dollars apiece for them…try me, rich person…no way. there's something about these guitars that when i look at 'em i feel that even though there is a lot of bad stuff going on in the world, maybe i can use these things to at least make someone smile or dance or think about stuff that matters every now and then... now i got a few new gibsons that i love too…a true vintage j45 that is just wonderful and a reissue 1943 southern jumbo and an advanced jumbo. codey and mark at gibson are the best people there are when it comes to getting great guitars into the hands of musicians. i also own a 1959 martin d18e…it has 2 dearmond pickups that the martin factory actually put on it…they only made 301 of them from 1959 and 1960 and the only other one i've ever seen was when kurt cobain played one on *mtv: unplugged*. it's a one trick pony but it's a good trick. my amps are a '59 fender vibrolux, two '63 fender brownface supers, a '64 princeton reverb, a '64 vibro champ, a '54 gibsonette, a '60 gibson ranger and a '51 bell & howell speaker cabinet with a stromberg/carlson amplifier from sometime way in the past. i use a medium glass rock slide and i have a coricidin bottle that belonged to gary stewart in a pill bottle with writing on it in his handwriting that says duane allman gave it to him but i have no proof of that. now lucas plays a gold top les paul of course, a sg that scott maddox from smoky mountain harley gave him and a 1937 137. all gibsons of course. now i got to mention collings…they are in dripping springs and their quality and sound is fantastic and are the best luthiers in texas that i know of…bill and his guys do a lot of great charity work also and i have used a collings on certain songs for that sonic sound they have…i used one on the song "moss and flowers" on *grifters hymnal.* oh yeah…let's not get out of here without plugging south austin music, hill country guitars, charley's guitars in dallas and… and…hmmm…estes audiology…they gave me my hearing back after too many years hearing that damn crash cymbal on a drum riser that was level with my left ear. you'll notice any drummer i use now doesn't have a crash cymbal. so gibson in boseman, i await your call. commercial is over. back to our program.

Old Guitar

Written by Ray Wylie Hubbard
Snake Farm Publishing (SESAC)

Got an old guitar I got me some licks I been piddling with
I got an old guitar I got me some licks I've been piddling with
I'm gonna write a song, I got some words I've been fiddling with

My guitar don't look like much but I love the way it plays
My guitar don't look like much but I love the way it plays
I know I ain't good looking, my woman loves me anyway

Give a boy a guitar he's going to play until his fingers bleed
Give a boy a guitar he's going to play until his fingers bleed
Got to raise him up right on Muddy, Lightnin', Hooker and Reed

Well I got an old guitar I got me some licks I been piddling with
I got an old guitar I got me some licks I been piddling with
I'm gonna write a song, I got some words I been fiddling with

chapter 10

The Outpost, Buffalo, Tony Joe

So I'd been doing Red River in the summers, North Texas State University in the fall, winter and spring, and playing and writing a few songs. Rick and Wayne and I, now known as Three Faces West, leased an abandoned building in Red River and founded the Outpost, serving lemonade, iced tea and coffee, and where we could play at night.

It was the first real coffeehouse in the area for young people, and it was a success; we had lines out the door.

One summer while sitting on the front porch of the Jeep Trailways office drinking chicory coffee and smoking a cigarette, someone passing through from Austin told me that Tony Joe White was playing the Chequered Flag club in Austin on a Wednesday in two weeks. So I called Rod Kennedy who ran the place and asked if I could open for him. He had only known me from Three Faces West, but I convinced him that solo I was as good as Michael Murphey; I wasn't.

On Wednesdays the Outpost was closed, so I figured I could leave Tuesday after we closed at 11 p.m., drive to Austin, get there about three in the afternoon, sleep a little, play the gig, meet and hear Tony Joe, leave about midnight and get back to Rio Rojo on Thursday to make the show at eight the next night.

When I started working on my set list, I realized it wasn't that long.

I had heard about this kid from Oklahoma who worked down at the pizza joint and had played lead guitar in a rock and roll band. I knew Rick and Wayne wouldn't want to go so I figured I'd ask him and with some extended guitar breaks we could do a 45 minute set.

So I walked into the pizza place and there's this skinny kid with glasses with hair down to the middle of his back washing dishes in the kitchen and smoking a cigarette.

"You want to go to Austin in a couple of weeks and play guitar with me to open for Tony Joe White?"

He took a drag off his cigarette, grabbed a plate, dunked it in the sink, began scrubbing it, exhaled smoke out of his nose and said, "No, I'd rather do this."

I took note of his sarcasm.

The next day he came down to the cabin Rick and I were staying in and we started rehearsing; he told me his name was Buffalo.

We left the following Tuesday night after the Outpost closed and headed for Austin. I got three diet pills from Riverview Café Jack's wife Edna to help with the drive.

We got to Amarillo about 5 a.m., filled up, Buffalo slept and I just kept on driving. I was just having a great time with the windows rolled down, the wind, the highway, and I think it was Hearts and Flowers on the cassette player. Then the sun started to come up in the rearview mirror and I was cruising right along. I was thinking, "It's beautiful out in West Texas at dawn," when I see a road sign that said, "Tucumcari 80 miles." Something was not right. It took me a few minutes to realize I was going west on 40 rather than east. I guess I wasn't paying that much attention after I filled up, or maybe thinking too fast might have had something to do with it. We turned around.

We got to Austin about four o'clock and met Tony Joe. He was and is one soulful cat. We played and then he just smoked the stage and left it in shreds.

We left about one a.m. after really hitting it off with Tony Joe. We did laugh. A lot.

Somewhere that morning north of Amarillo, I stopped and waited for a train to pass. Buffalo woke up and asked me what I was doing parked on the highway.

"I'm waiting for this train to pass."

"There is no train. Get out, I'm driving."

I wasn't even sleepy. He took over and we drove straight to the Outpost. He dropped me off about 7 p.m. On stage that night were Two Faces West and one dead-ass zombie.

But I'd met Tony Joe White.

rwh

i am recording at gurf's and playing resonator and my brass slide hits a fret and i stop. gurf's voice comes through the headphones and asks, why did you stop?
i say my slide hit the wood.
after a few seconds he says, lightnin' hopkins wouldn't have stopped.
a few moments later he continues, the eagles would have.
now i gotta lot of respect for the eagles but i know i don't have the capacity to make a record like that.
what he was teaching me was that performance is as important as perfection.
the lightnin' albums, even where he was out of tune, are just as perfect as the eagles i believe.
now if i had an unlimited budget and my choice of any producer in the world to work with on an album, i would choose either lloyd maines, gurf morlix or george reiff, you read that right, over anybody else.
recording with those guys i felt like prometheus stealing fire from the gods. what i came away with was, it comes down to grit, groove, tone and taste, as well as being honest, open minded and willing.
not gonna get into a technical thing about each album i did with them, but if you listen to my records...well, you may not care for the singer or the songs, but you can't deny that they sound cool.

chapter 11

The Cowboy Twinkies, Fast Times

One night I showed up at the Outpost to play after I'd been drinking. I was in no condition to perform. I wasn't in a blackout but was stumbling, slurring my words and I could not play the guitar. Rick and Wayne raked me over the coals afterwards as they had every right to. As they were berating me I was remorseful and apologizing; I said it would never happen again. I remember thinking, I hope this ends before the bars close.

I pulled it together for the rest of the summer. But the writing was on the wall. Rick and Wayne were going to stay in Red River and I was going to continue to drink. Wayne had gotten married and was doing some construction work as a contractor, and Rick was doing art and skiing and I was doing gigs with Buffalo in Dallas, Austin, etc. (This is where it starts to get confusing and I don't have a time frame for what follows.)

I moved back to Dallas and I think I moved back in with my folks.

I ran into Pat Toomay of the Dallas Cowboys at a club and we became friends. Some Cowboys had opened a club/sports bar in Fort Worth and he told me he could get me a gig there but I'd need a band. I called Buffalo and told him this. He says he knows a drummer and a bass player who doesn't talk.

They came down to rehearse and I was introduced to drummer Jim Herbst and bass player Dennis Meehan. Oh yeah, the gig was that night.

We set up in my folk's living room and I said something like, "Let's just do some simple, standard songs to get us through the gig."

I play about half of "Lonesome Fugitive," by Merle Haggard and everybody falls in and it sounds pretty good. I asked if everybody got it. Jim and Buff said yeah, and Dennis just looked at me. We do "Long Black Veil," and it's the same thing. Dennis doesn't talk. We go over "Whiskey River." Not a word from the bass player. We learned seven songs and I said we ought to come up with a name for the band so they know it's not just me doing a solo, you know like Ray Wylie Hubbard and the whatever.

Dennis startled me. The first words out of his mouth were: "I always wanted to be in a band called 'the Twinkies'." I said, "Well, since we're in Fort Worth we might ought to be the Cowboy Twinkies." The second thing Denis said was, "just so you know, my stage name is Clovis Robilaine." It was agreed upon.

We got to the gig and there is another band playing first. We set up our amps and drums and were going to share equipment. We were in the dressing room when they started. Their first song was "Whiskey River," and then they did "Lonesome Fugitive."

I panicked. They did two songs that we had planned our set on. Now we got "Long Black Veil," "Redneck Mother," "Muddy Boggy Banjo Man," "Long Lonely Day," and that's it, man.

Jimmy says "I can do "Wipeout" and go into "Communication Breakdown." Buff offered "Purple Haze." Dennis doesn't say anything.

I said, "Buff, let's do "Lonesome Fugitive," but do the lead break like Hendrix. And Jimmy, you get a drum solo in "Long Black Veil." Dennis...sorry, uh, Clovis, I'll describe what you're wearing like a fashion show so walk around like a model. We'll do "Muddy Boggy" second, and then do it again next to last, but in a different key and half-ass reggae. We do "Redneck Mother" as a sing-along, and let them sing the chorus over and over 'till they get bored and quit, and then we'll just walk off."

They loved us. Of course they were drunk but, well, you know.

Things were happening fast now: Willie Nelson's house in Nashville burned down and he moved to Austin, as did Jerry Jeff Walker. Michael Murphey was in L.A. and did a TV pilot about young civil war rock and rollers with Boomer Castleman. And Louis Charles Stevenson III was now known as B.W. Stevenson and had a record deal. Gram Parsons was taking a rock and roll attitude toward country. Eddie Wilson bought an armory and opened the Armadillo World Headquarters in South Austin. Waylon Jennings was getting shaggy and lowdown. A guy named Gino McCoslin got fired from the straight western place nightclub in Dallas and opened one with 57 old doors nailed to the wall and called it what else? 57 Doors. Bill Simonson opened Mother Blues and booked Lightnin' Hopkins and Jimmy Buffett. The folk club called the Rubaiyat was rolling along. Townes Van Zandt was mesmerizing people at the Old Quarter in Houston. Rusty Wier, Layton DePenning and John Inmon were working a lot in Austin with bands like Freda and the Firedogs, Denim, and Frummox, and solo musicians Alan Damron, the great Johnny Vandiver, Big Bill Moss, Guy Clark, and the kid, Willis Alan Ramsey, were all throwing down. It was long hair, weed, music, Lone Star beer, braless hippie girls with braided hair, cowboys boots, straw hats, work shirts with patches and embroidery, country songs with loud nasty tones, rock songs with steel guitar licks, folk songs with a backbeat, mescaline, beards, antiwar protests, sunglasses at night, do-what-we-want attitude, and worth mentioning again, braless hippie girls with braided hair.

Everybody was getting a record deal.

We went into Pecan Street Studios on Sixth Street in Austin, with Chet Himes engineering and we started recording. Even though we were Ray Wylie Hubbard and the Cowboy Twinkies, I thought of myself as a folk singer with drums, bass and electric guitar. I was confused, torn between two worlds. I was writing these songs that I thought were folkie acoustic, but the shows were becoming wild, enthusiastic crazy Hendrix-Led Zep-type events. We tracked 10 songs. Pat Toomay started shopping them around as we had no manager and we got offers from everybody, including Frank Zappa's DiscReet Records.

Pat and I flew to New York and met Atlantic Records president Jerry Wexler and had dinner at his high-rise penthouse apartment overlooking Central Park. The next night he gave us his tickets to see Bruce Springsteen perform at the Bottom Line, which was the Tuesday that *Greetings from Asbury Park* was released.

It seemed everybody loved the tape of the songs we did, but wanted to re-record them. We signed with Atlantic. Bob Johnston was enlisted to produce. We went to Muscle Shoals and were going to record with their staff players along with Buffalo, Jimmy and Dennis (Clovis).

When we got to the studio, Bob started smoking grass. I played him the songs that were on our tape and he said, "What else you got?" I didn't have anything else. To me it seemed that the songs were good enough to get us a record deal.

Bob suggested other songs by writers he knew. I started to get this queasy feeling that became full-tilt terror in the pit of my stomach. I felt like I wasn't ready to do this. Not this way.

I could not get in touch with Toomay because he was in training camp, so I called Jerry Wexler at home. He was having a dinner party for Bette Midler and wasn't too happy that I'd disturbed him.

I explained that I was playing and singing "Portales," when Bob interrupted me and went to the piano and played a song he had written. I sang "Border Town Girl" and Bob stopped me. He felt it wasn't strong enough. I couldn't understand it. We got a lot of requests for the song when we played live. The same thing happened with "West Texas Dance Band."

Mr. Wexler said, "Maybe you're just not ready yet."

I agreed.

We flew out the next morning without even calling Johnston to tell him. He showed up at the studio that day and we didn't.

Today I regret the way I handled that situation. My response then was, "fuck it." It was immature and unprofessional. I still believe Bob Johnston just couldn't get the idea of this folk-rock album we were trying to do, and maybe he was right that the songs weren't good enough, but there was this uncomfortable vibe permeating the experience. Being in the studio, him rolling a joint and then, during a song I'm singing, he gets up and just walks out of the room or goes to the piano and starts singing something else.

Mr. Wexler was gracious to let me out of the contract even after incurring all the expense. Neither man deserved my rude and amateur behavior.

For 35 years, the memory of this horrible, embarrassing thing I had done was always lurking in the corners and shadows of my poor old brain, without hope of it ever being resolved.

In 2005, about six months after *Delirium Tremolos* came out, I received a post card from Florida with a picture of Sleepy John Estes on one side. On the other side was a handwritten note that said:

Dear Ray,

Delirium *knocked me out. Dynamite in all respects: rhythm section, material, vocals plus a really great mix. Pianist Dick Hyman laid this line on me. "When in doubt, tremolo!" Congrats!*

— Jerry Wexler

I wrote him back and said I was wrong for the way I behaved and asked what could I do to make an amends for that injustice. After a week or so, a handwritten letter arrived from Jerry telling me that the slate had been wiped clean because I had made a great record.

Dust of the Chase

Written by Ray Wylie Hubbard
Snake Farm Publishing (SESAC)

I come down from Oklahoma with a pistol in my boot
A pair of dice, a deck of cards, and a Bible in my suit
I come here as the cause of tears, just a crying shame
Seven stud or eternal blood, I'm looking for a game

I double-crossed the state of Texas and they give me a little time
I taught myself to double cut the cards and hold Scriptures in my mind
I learned to love the tumbling dice and to believe the Word
Tombstones and rolling bones, beats anything I ever heard

Patience is a virtue that I don't possess
And I can't deny that Heaven lies beneath a cotton dress
How small a part of time we share till we hear the sound of wings
I am lost in the dust of the chase that my life brings

I have walked through God's green pastures and beneath his rich blue skies
I've seen the fall of man and the Kingdom hidden from their eyes
I have heard the roar of thunder; I felt a lightening bolt
And when I walk through the Valley of the Shadow of Death I take along Samuel Colt

Every night I kiss the cards and hold them to my breast
And when I see the King of Hearts, I know that I am blessed
And though my eyes are blind sometimes I know there's something there
So when the time's at hand and I kill a man, I say a little prayer

rwh

there was a biker swap meet i played when i was about 40 or 45, which was a front for a meeting of the hell's angels, the bandidos and the scorpions up near gainesville.

scott mathews is now the great drummer for the derailers but at the time he was scotty mathews and it was his first gig with me and he was like 16 and we had to get his parents' okay and he showed up to play this biker fest in khaki shorts and a button down ralph lauren shirt and like these white yacht shoes.

jon mastin was on bass and when we got there he didn't take any crap off these guys at all. he jumped out of the van and said, hey we need some meat over here to unload our gear. 4 or 5 old boys came over and helped get the amps and drums unloaded.

so there's about 50 bikers from each club…we didn't know this at the time…the guy who hired us left that part out. seems the angels wanted to come to texas and the bike swap meet was a cover for the negotiations… also there were about 15 or so dentists or lawyers or insurance salesmen who had harleys that just showed up because of the swap meet.

about halfway through our set, the talks broke down and three different sets of 50 bikes went roaring out of the abandoned drive-in theater where the "swap meet" was being held.

so we were left to play the last 30 minutes to middle-aged mild mannered men who owned motorcycles… we had actually learned and rehearsed "born to be wild," but it just wasn't the same playing it for 15 guys that before we began our set one of 'em told scotty he had really nice teeth and a couple of 'em wanted to sell jon insurance.

chapter 12

Rope Letters, Self Will; Run Riot

So we had this tape and the music scene was passing us by. We were playing and selling out the same venues Willie, Jerry Jeff and B.W. were playing, and recording, but couldn't get our record out. Michael Brodsky approached us and offered to produce an album. We were a band so we wanted to record as one.

We went to Nashville, recorded the same songs with the same guys, and the same arrangements, and then we hit the road. Michael took the tape to the Reprise office in Nashville and the way I understood it was that they told him that country radio wouldn't play it because it was a folk-rock record. So the label put rope letters on this work-in-progress cover art, and put Jet and the Jewels' ooohing and aaaahing backing vocals on all the tracks so it would suck.

They mailed us a cassette of the *finished* album, which was news to us. We couldn't believe what we were hearing. We were literally holding back tears while listening. My mom came home from work and walked up to the van and saw how despondent we were, and asked, "What's the matter?"

"We're listening to our new record."

I called Pat Toomay, hysterical. I called my lawyer and asked him what I could do about it. He advised me to start drinking because there was nothing else to do. So I did, until November 13, 1987.

I got an apartment about two blocks from 57 Doors. We were still filling up clubs and gigging everywhere. I was playing and getting drunk, doing pills and cocaine and playing poker with Freddie King,* Bugs Henderson, John Nitzinger and Bill Simonson, upstairs at Mother Blues after hours. I was running with girls with names like Tuesday Night, Bubbles Cash, Dixie Cup and Brandy Wine. They danced and took their clothes off at seedy nightclubs. I was on top of the world.

I was starting to get sick and seemed to be throwing up a lot, so I switched to Brandy Alexanders and Black Russians, but ended up in the hospital anyway. They ran some tests. I was 29 years old and the doctor told me I had pancreatitis and needed to quit drinking.

I say, "like hard liquor?"

"You need to quit *drinking*."

"You don't mean beer. Beer's okay right?"

"You have to quit drinking or you'll die."

Desperate, I asked him, "how about a glass of wine with dinner? Surely that's alright, isn't it?"

He says, "you can have a glass of wine every other week."

I'm relieved.

"As long I don't have to quit drinking."

So I quit drinking, got married and had a son.

The marriage fell apart after six years but I loved that boy and I still do.

There is a phrase that describes pretty much the way it was after the divorce: self will, run riot. Yep.

As I have said, the time frame on this is nowhere near accurate. Even if I knew the exact dates for all this, I doubt it would add anything to your reading experience except some numbers. It's pretty much a fog and ragged memories that don't make a lot of sense anyway, so knowing what year this stuff happened in will not make this read any smoother. It'll just clog things up.

Willie Nelson's contract was coming up for renewal with CBS so Polygram offered him his own label if he signed with them. So he started Lone Star Records and signed his friends and fellow Texas songwriters: there's me, Milton Carroll, Billy Calarey, Cooder Browne, Steve Fromholz, and the Geezinslaws.

He told me he needed something out quick, and asked if I had anything. I told him I had some demos, but they were all over the place; some in Tyler, some in Dallas, some in Austin.

He tells me he needs them fast 'cause he is doing a 38-city tour in January and I can open for him if I can get the tapes to his people the following Monday so we'll have them for the tour. He really wants "Redneck Mother" on the album, too. I didn't want to do it but saying no to Willie would be like blowing smoke in God's face.

So I drove all over Texas getting these demo tapes. Then I grabbed George M. Jones (not George Jones, the possum), Larry White, my band, and the Mother Of Pearl Band and went into a studio in Dallas on Friday. I overdubbed, sang, recorded, mixed and mastered the songs, borrowed a shirt, took a picture, and drove the negative and the master recording out to Love Field Airport Monday afternoon and gave them to someone who flew them to Nashville for pressing.

The lone condition I gave Willie was that I would do all this if, for the next record, I could have a budget, a producer and some time. He said, "You got it."

We played a drive-in theater in Houston with Willie to start the tour. Someone threw a beer can toward the stage and it just missed him. The people in the crowd saw this guy and picked him up and lifted him over the barricade, then handed him to security. Paul English quit playing drums, came down off the stage, hit him in the face and knocked him out. Then they threw him over the fence, back into the crowd and he just laid there. Paul went back up onstage and got behind the drum kit; the crowd cheered.

We got in our van and drove to Fargo for the next gig. We played 38 cities in 40 days throughout the Midwest and northeast. We played Michigan, Wisconsin, and South Dakota during January and February. It was cold! Our record didn't come out until March, after the tour was over. So not only were we unable to exploit the tour to sell records, we just seemed to piss people off who had to wait for us to quit playing so they could see Willie.

* Freddie's favorite game was Loosy Duecy: A seven-card stud game in which whatever card came face up after a deuce was wild.

Mississippi Flush

Written by Ray Wylie Hubbard
Snake Farm Publishing (SESAC)

Well they got a little game called Five Card Draw
They take it serious in Arkansas
You can make a little money wagering on cards
You can't get to Heaven living this hard
Deliver me from my sorrow and shame
Release me from my burden and pain

It's a One Eyed Jack and a Suicide King
Ace of spades and two black queens
Never draw to an inside straight
I feel a ten knocking at the gate
Deliver me from my sorrow and shame
Release me from my burden and pain

Blackbird, blackbird fly away home
Say a prayer over St. John's bones
Tell the gamblers they're gonna die alone
Blackbird, blackbird fly away home

Blackbird, blackbird come back again
Don't tell mamma where I been
Going to the river and I'm gonna jump in
Blackbird, blackbird come back again

It's an Ace High Straight and all the same suit
Read 'em and weep this hand can't lose
Somebody said "That ain't good enough,
That don't beat a Mississippi Flush"

"Mr. Ledbetter will you tell me again
What's a Mississippi Flush and how's it beat this hand?"
He said "They don't ask questions in the graveyard
It's a small revolver and any five cards"

rwh

so the door buzzer buzzes in my apartment about 3 in the morning. it buzzes again and just stays buzzing. i had fallen asleep on the couch so i get up and i go over and push a button.
who is it?
hubbard, its poodie and michael jean and paul english.
i walk back over and set down on the couch, light a cigarette and the buzzer buzzes and buzzes and buzzes and i walk back over to the wall and against my better judgement i hit the door release button.
the three men who belong to the voices on my intercom come stumbling in.
we're going to milwaukee to play a beer fest. we're playing a beer fest, hubbard. It's a dream come true. It's a beer fest and it's in milwaukee. do you have any drugs?
i have some. we do some.
i am now wide awake with two wild ass hellions from willie nelson's road crew and his great drummer with a felon under my melon.
come on and go with us...it's a beer fest. we gonna meet willie on the time tube* in garland and head to a beer fest.
i can't man, i got tickets to the eagles and this girl i been trying to sleep with loves the eagles and this dj friend of mine got me really good tickets and i think me taking her to their concert will seal the sex act deal.
aw man, they sound just like their records. we going to a beer fest...in milwaulkee.
sorry, i can't.
after a few minutes and a lot of talking fast it's now 6 am and poodie picks me up by my feet and michael jean picks me up by my hands and they carry me down the stairs and paul grabs my old black leather coat and says you can borrow willie's toothbrush. we kidnapping your ass. they put me in the back seat of this buick i think it was and off we go.
i think they are kidding.
we drive to garland and they carry me up the stairs on this old bus that has been converted with bunks and couches and someone gets off the bus and gets in the buick i think it was and drives off. the door close and we are rolling on i30 out of dallas.
sometime that afternoon we stop at a truck stop and i

call back on a pay phone to the girl and say i think i'm in tulsa and she says where are the tickets and i say on the coffee table in my apartment and she hangs up and the sex act deal was to remain unsealed.

so along the way we had run out of cocaine (and at this time let me say i never saw willie do any. ever. poodie and i did. a lot. and quite often)...so at the truck stop we buy a bunch of stuff like beanie weenies, chips, beer, ice and cope. cope was a women's menstrual pain reliever in the '70s. poodie gets on the bus and proceeds to crush it and chop it up into a fine powder. he says ray, care for some copaine? i say sure. i knew it probably wouldn't get me high but it was the loving of the game.

we get to milwaukee and it was a beer fest.

for some reason during the trip in the middle of the night rolling down some interstate i remember paul pulled out a .22 derringer and yelled "homer, i'm gonna shoot" and then fired into either a phone book or a gideon bible as i was near passed out on the floor and at some other point in the odyssey bee spears nailed the door to the bathroom closed for some reason and then bit my ear almost off wrestling and someone put a pillow case over my head and kept blowing pot into it thought a little hole with a straw and we got there and willie played the beer fest and we came back through somewhere like chicago and jerry jeff was playing some club and willie's family had torn me up so much that i jumped off the time tube and thought it would be better for my health and much safer to hang with jerry jeff walker. this decision alone proves that i was never mensa material.

*they called willie's bus 'the time tube' cause you got on it at one place and after a period of time you got off of it and you were someplace else. also there was a stick tied to a string hanging from a nail in the roof. it was magical paul said... it told you remarkable things...like if it was wet, you were under water, if it was touching the roof, you were upside down, if it was on fire...well, you get the picture...it was magical.

chapter 13

Low Chicago, Blackouts

I was in Austin when my dad died. He had a stroke. I buried him next to my mom in the Hugo, Oklahoma cemetery.

Now my dad's favorite poker game was Low Chicago; which is seven card stud and the low spade in the hole gets half the pot. One of my favorite pictures is of him and Bugs Henderson playing cards and Bugs has turned over the 6 of spades and my dad has turned over the 4 of spades. Right before they closed the casket at the funeral, Bugs slipped a 2 of spades into my dad's lapel suit pocket so that he would always split the pot whenever there was a card game in the hereafter.

I was 38 years old and an orphan now. Johnny and Jerry Crawford helped me through this time and I appreciated all they did for me, but the grieving process was horrendous, even alcohol couldn't dull the terrible emptiness. I went through the money from my dad's life insurance in about a year. Besides buying cocaine and drinking with impunity, I bought an old GMC 4104 bus. Of the three it's hard to say which was the worst decision.

The loss of my dad put me in a nosedive. Terry Ware, Dan Kinney, John Inmon, Bob Livingston, Paul Pearcy, Bugs Henderson, Bobby Chitwood, and Ron Thompson were great and patient friends during this time. There were also a bunch of hangers on (who were probably nice when they were children, but had grown into lowlifes and swindlers and dopers and bad drunks like me) crashing at the house my dad had left me.

One night I was partying with professional tag team wrestlers Kerry Von Erich and Gentleman Chris Adams along with Walker Carver who was my favorite drug dealer — well, except for Ron McKeown. They got to showing me some wrestling holds, and then Kerry put me in a headlock and wouldn't let me out. Brian tells him to let me go. He won't. Then they get in this yelling match. Kerry let me go, then he and Brian start wrestling and fighting for real in Walker's apartment and it was pretty scary. I think it was the next Friday at the Sportatorium that Chris betrayed Von Erich and turned heel.

I had moved back into the house I had grown up in in Oak Cliff. My exwife D'Ann, my son Cory and her new husband David were living in Seagoville.

I was going down the drain.

I was in this make believe world I had created for myself. It was a dark kingdom where I thought of myself as a Keith Richards cool drug rocker, a Townes Van Zandt tortured songwriter, a Dylan Thomas heartbroken poet. The reality was that I was just a sloppy blackout drunk playing, "Up Against the Wall, Redneck Mother," twice a night in these shitty honk tonks and seedy bars in Fort Worth and Dallas and Oklahoma, where the patrons drank like I did. Offstage, I thought I was doing this Don Rickles' funny, witty insult humor, when in reality I was just saying mean and hurtful things to people.

I thought cocaine was the answer to my drinking problem but it just gave my booze legs.

I owned a 9mm Walther, a .38 caliber Smith & Wesson, a couple of Ruger .22 pistols, and a .32 caliber Beretta. I liked to take a fifth of J.T.S. Brown whiskey and an eight ball of cocaine and drive around with 'em by myself. For what purpose I had no idea.

I came out one morning and someone had shot out the passenger window of my van. I wondered who had done it 'til I looked and there were a couple of bullet holes in the passenger door from the inside. I had no recollection of doing that. I had done it while in a blackout. It was getting to the point I was blacking out about every other time I drank.

I was pretty miserable…take out 'pretty,' and put in 'goddam.'

I'd come to not being able to remember what I did but then if I did remember, overwhelming remorse would bore its way into and gnaw at my conscience till I could drink enough to blot it out.

Darkness had swooped down on me and I was completely lost within my own skin.

It got to the point I thought about killing myself yet couldn't actually follow through despite the fact I knew I couldn't continue to live like I was living. And I knew I couldn't continue to drink like I was drinking yet I couldn't stop drinking.

So there I was: I couldn't live. I couldn't die. I couldn't drink. I couldn't quit drinking.

Voila: AA.

Didn't Have A Prayer

Written by Ray Wylie Hubbard
Snake Farm Publishing (SESAC)

I used to take comfort
From the loneliness with whiskey
It tore up my soul
And it turned against me
I stood at the fire with my hand on the knife
Didn't have a prayer to save my life

I stood at the crossroads with tears in my eyes
I'd come as far as I could bring me
I could not live and I could not die
There was darkness all around me, no sun up in the sky
Didn't have a prayer to save my life

I wasn't looking for something to fall from the sky
I'd come to believe just what I see with my eyes
I wasn't looking for nothing but love from the start
I need to get me, I got to find me, I got to have me
A little peace in my heart

I stood in spiritual rags
Blinded by the dust of pride
Poisoned by my own cold, cold heart
And the shallow reign of my life
In the distance there was thunder
I saw the lightning strike twice
I threw out a little prayer
I threw out a little prayer
Threw out a little prayer
Not expecting a reply

rwh

so i played the choctaw casino south of hugo where i was born and i thought nobody would show up but it was packed out. hometown boy made good or at least adequate enough to draw about a thousand people in choctaw county in the rain. the mayor of hugo and the city manager gave me the key to the city but i couldn't get it off the plaque to see if it would open any pawn shop doors in hugo after midnight.

so the next day judy and i go out to mount olive cemetery where my folks are buried and i also show her where the circus folks are buried with ringmasters and elephant headstones.

then we head over to soper and see a small herd of buffalo. we stop and there among them is a white one. not like bleached white shiny white but it's white. judy took some pictures of it and some headstones and the house i started off in there in soper and the front porch from where i stood and threw a rock and hit my cousin in the head. we drove by the first baptist church where i was baptized and noticed they now have indoor restrooms.

Conversation With The Devil

Written by Ray Wylie Hubbard
Snake Farm Publishing (SESAC)

I had a dream last night I was cast into hell by a jealous God
The devil walked up and said "You won't need no lightning rod
It hardly ever rains down here, I can't recall the last storm.
You're not gonna need that leather jacket, it gets kind of warm.
There's one way in, no way out, looks like you're here to stay.
The place is a mess, it's over crowded and more are coming in every day"

I said, "Awe man, wait a minute, there's got to be something wrong.
I ain't a bad guy, I just write these little songs
I always pay my union dues, and I don't stay in the passing lane."
He said," What about all that whiskey and cocaine?"
I said, "Well, sure man, but that no reason to throw me in hell.
I didn't use the cocaine to get high, I just liked the way it smelled."

He said "Come over here son let me show you around.
Over there's where we put the preachers; I never liked those clowns.
They're always blaming me for everything wrong under the sun
It's not harder to do what's right, its just maybe not as much fun.
They walk around thinking they're better than me and you
And then they get caught in a motel room doing what they said not to do."

"Now all the murders and rapists go into a fiery lake
As well as most of the politicians and cops on the take
And all the mothers who wait till they get to K-Mart to spank their kids

Instead of showing them what to do what's right, they just hit them for what they did.
And all the daddies who run off and abandon their daughters and sons
Anybody who hurts a child is gonna burn until they're done."

"Every body's down here," I said, "who's up in Heaven with God and His Son?"
"Oh some saints and mystics and students of metaphysics 101
People who care and share and love and try to do what's right
Beautiful old souls who read little stories to their babies every night.
What you won't find up in Heaven are Christian Coalition Right Wing Conservatives
Country program directors and Nashville record executives."

I said "I made some mistakes but I'm not as bad as those guys
How can God do this to me can't you sympathize?"
He said, "You're wrong about God being cruel and mean
God is the most loving thing that's never been seen."
"Well, hot shot," I said, "Tell me this which religion is the truest?"
He said, "They're all the same, Buddha was not a Christian, but Jesus would have made a good Buddhist."

I thought about my future and I didn't seem to have much of one
Looked around to leave but there was no place to run
I said, "I don't suppose I could go back and try living again
You know like reincarnation, I hear that's the way it's always been."
"I can't answer that," he said "You'll have to wait for that response
But it's not any more unusual to be born twice than it is to be born once."

It looked like I was gonna be stuck here as far as I could tell
I thought I might as well suck up; what the hell
I said, "You know that song that Charlie Daniel's did

About how you went down to Georgia and played fiddle against that kid?"
"Yeah," he said "It broke my heart, but what are you gonna do?"
I said, "Well to tell you the truth I thought your solo was the better of the two."

Then I woke up and I was lying in my bed
I ran up the stairs and kissed my little boy on his sleeping head
I took this dream as a sign from God so I thought I better pray
I said, "Don't ever speak to me directly and thanks anyway."
Now so much has changed about me besides just giving up red meat
Some get spiritual cause they see the light and some cause they feel the heat.

chapter 14

Stevie, A Conversation in Purgatory

"There ain't no elevators, you got to take the steps," Stevie Ray and B.C. said almost together.

I felt I was about to jump out of my skin. I hadn't had a drink or a rail of coke in over 24 hours. I sat across from them and mumbled, "This is intense."

They seemed not to hear me. "You want to quit drinking?" "Yeah, that's why I'm talking to you guys." "Well, the first thing you do is quit drinking." "Well, I can't. That's why I'm, talking to..." "If you want to quit drinking, the first thing you do is quit drinking." "If I could quit drinking, I wouldn't be here talking to..." "The first thing you do if you want to quit drinking is quit drinking."

I was in some fucked up Abbott and Costello purgatory. I was shaking and getting no sympathy from one of the best guitar players on the planet and his "sponsor," whatever the hell that was. I thought that this was a grave mistake, 'cause they said I had to quit drinking in order to quit drinking. This was some fucked up shit. But the dancer/actress I'd been seeing for a while had been sober six months and even though we had broken up, she had set up this whatever it was, face-to-face thing after Stevie had spoken at a hospital AA meeting. "So you quit drinking first, and then work the 12 steps of AA like the book says, and then you have a spiritual awakening, and as long as you do certain things on a daily basis, you don't drink," one said.

"But it's just one day at a time." I floated in and out of the conversation, my thinking going like slot cars without the slots. I was all over the spectrum of mind fuckedupness, coming down and off. I was confused and didn't know what I was thinking let alone what the hell they were talking about.

The last time I had seen Stevie Ray had been in Austin like in 1982 or '83 at Riverside Studios at 10 a.m. after I had been up all night, and he'd been up 30-something hours mixing his record. We were talking fast, not making sense, drinking hard liquor and sharing coke, so I knew he drank and did drugs like I did. Now here he was in November of 1987, 14 months sober.

rwh

so i was 25, 26 years old living in red river n. m. in the 70s and jerry jeff comes into town on a wednesday and everybody is so excited. everyone's going, hey your friend is the guy that wrote "mr. bojangles." he's like a star and we never met a famous songwriter before and he's famous and he's here in town and wow, we're so happy to have the guy who wrote the nitty gritty dirt band's big hit song right here in our town and this is great for the community and boy howdy, this is so cool having jerry jeff staying in our town.

by friday, people were coming up to me saying, when…ah...do you think your friend is going to leave?

i think it might have been bud shrake who said there are people on the earth older than jerry jeff but he's been awake longer.

somewhere round 1980 the lost gonzo band (paul pearcy, john inmon and bob livingston) left jerry jeff and became my band…they didn't know it at the time but in hindsight it's kinda like they just traded for a different seat on the titantic.

no lifeboats here.

we did have some great gigs and had some wild adventures and exciting times…there's nothing quite like waking up on a 4104 bus that you had taken all the seats out but hadn't built any bunks in it yet so you're on the floor in a sleeping bag and you hear the bus pull off to the side of the road and then you hear gary mac the driver shout, "abandon bus! run for it!" or you're driving on the golden gate bridge going into san francisco and you ask him why that gauge on the dash is acting funny and he says, "i think that there means we don't have any brakes" or you're parked outside the lone star cafe in nyc and the windows are open cause the ac don't work and you're waking up to people who are sticking their heads in the windows to just look around.

oh yeah. it was the big time.

what else?

oh yeah back to jjw.

donny brooks sold me a 1938 roy smeck stage delux with an angel painted on it and "babe" carved in the top for $250 under the condition i could never sell it to anyone but him or jerry jeff.

five years later i was playing it in the last run bar in

red river one night when jerry jeff walked in. i tried to slide it down and pick up another guitar but he saw it. he said lemme borrow it and wrote "that beat up old guitar" on it and said he had to have it back. he traded me a $1200 guild for it that never stayed in tune and then i traded that to seigel frye for a dobro and then traded that for a martin d21 and then traded that for a gibson j160 and then traded that for a 59 martin d18e that i still got. It's like the one kurt cobain played on *mtv unplugged*. it's pretty gnarly.

As I wrote earlier, my favorite guitar is a 1959 gibson southern jumbo body with a 1949 j45 neck that's got a dearmond toaster top pickup on it behind the sound hole. And lemme mention again luthier tony nobles of the devil's backbone guitar co. did the work.

it's old and funky...but hey, so am i.

old and funky beats new and unfunky in my book... which is what you're reading so it must be the gospel truth.

speaking of funky, this is as good a time as any to tell how cool tony joe white is.

tony joe went to bat for me to his publishers so i could use "polk salad annie" in my song "mother blues." I used two lines from his song in my song so judy wrote emi to get permission and they wrote back and said they wanted 5000 dollars and 66 & 2/3 percent of the publishing of my song "mother blues." judy wrote them back (and I this is a direct quote) "fuck you, we'll bleep it out." I called tony joe and told him what they said and he said lemme call them old boys. The next day we got an email from emi saying we coud use it for free. tony joe is a stand up guy...except when he plays...then he sets down. he plugs his strat into a wah wah pedal into a blues deville and when he does...well the devil smiles and angels dance cause everybody digs a deep groove.

he lays it down so solid you could hammer nails with it. if that don't make him cool enough, he's got a snake skin guitar strap that actually still has the snake head on it that's got fangs made out of 14 caret gold. lord have mercy.

Snake Farm

Written by Ray Wylie Hubbard
Snake Farm Publishing (SESAC)

Well the woman I love is named Ramona
She kind of looks like Tempest Storm
She can dance like Little Egypt
And she works down at the Snake Farm

Snake Farm, it just sounds nasty
Snake Farm, it pretty much is
Snake Farm, it's a reptile house
Snake Farm…ooooooghhhhh

Ramona's got a keen sense of humor
She's got a tattoo down her arm
It's of a python eatin' a little mouse
With a sailor hat that says "Snake Farm"

I asked Ramona how come she works there
She said "Well it's got its charm"
There's nothing to do in the winter
And every now and then some kid gets bit at the Snake Farm

Ramona likes her malt liquor
And a band from Wales called The Alarm
She said she cried when they broke up
She still plays their records down at the Snake Farm

Sometimes Ramona calls me up
And says "Come on down here it's gettin' warm"
She runs every body off
And we…you know at the Snake Farm

chapter 15

Duke, An Agnostic's prayer

So Duke says, "Boys, I'm not going to be here next week. I am to appear before the judge Monday and since this is my third offense, my lawyer says I am going to do some time. I have enjoyed knowing you all and being a part of this men's step study group. These three months have been the longest I have stayed sober since I became a FTDD.*

I said, "Duke, man, I am sorry you're going to prison. You really have helped me a lot."

He pulled out a preamble from the basket and replied, "I'm not going to prison. I am going to become a fugitive in Mexico. Alcoholic Anonymous is a fellowship…"

My thoughts flew back to when I came through the door of the Phoenix Group last November. I pulled into the parking at the corner of Walnut Hill and Marsh Lane. There was a Hasty liquor store on one corner, a Centennial liquor store on the opposite corner and the group was upstairs over the Pilot Lounge and the Loft Lounge, which was next to a Marine recruiting office. I sat in my truck watching these people walk past all these places and was really impressed they could do that. I took a drag off my Bull Durham ready-rolled cigarette, and said to myself, "Well, if Stevie did it. I guess I can." Opening the door, I got out and walked up the stairs.

A man stood by the door and said, "I'm Doc, we're glad you're here." I don't remember much of what was said that night but I remember they laughed a lot and I hadn't laughed in a long, long time.

I wasn't an atheist when I walked up those stairs but I was a pretty militant agnostic. I thought an agnostic was someone who didn't know if there was a God or not. Later it was brought to my attention that an agnostic was someone who hadn't put forth the time and effort to find out.

After the meeting, Doc and a couple of guys cornered me and gave me this big blue book and said, "let's go to Denny's." As we sat in the booth one of the men said, "now in this book it starts off with this thing called 'The Doctor's Opinion.' If you read that, it will answer the two questions that you've been asking yourself that you don't have an answer for: one is 'how come I can't drink like I used to and have it be fun?' And the other question is, 'now that I want to quit, how come I can't?'"

It was like a hydrogen bomb went off in my head because I had been really asking myself that. I used to drink and it was fun, but now when I drank it wasn't fun, it was dangerous. And so many times I had told myself after coming to, not remembering what happened the night before, that I was quitting. Then I got drunk.

Doc looked at me and says, "He's all on fire about this 'cause Joe and Charlie spoke at Aquarius group last Saturday."

The man continued, "If you want to stay sober, every morning when you wake up ask God to keep you sober and if you stay sober, thank him at night."

"Well I don't go to church and don't really believe in God and I..."

"Doesn't matter. You ask God to keep you sober in the morning and thank him at night."

"Well, I don't believe in...."

"Doesn't matter what you believe. You just do it anyway."

"Don't you have to believe in God to pray?"

"It works better if you do, but you don't have to. God doesn't really need to hear your prayers. You need to hear yourself praying."

I went home that night and paced back and forth in this empty old house I had grown up in. I remembered my grandmother in Oklahoma taking me to church, and the people shouting and hollering, and the people being possessed by the Holy Spirit, and how terrified I was by the screaming and how crazy it was. I remembered people's faces in Soper back when I was baptized as a kid, and I thought to myself: did I really want to do this?

Doc and these old men I went to dinner with seemed pretty rational and they said they prayed. For a moment I thought, "Fuck it, let's go get some whiskey." I went and got my truck keys and stood in the kitchen for a long time. I put the keys on the counter, turned off the lights, and for the first time in about 25 years I got down on my knees and prayed. I said, "God, don't ever speak to me directly..."

I came out of my recollections and looked at the eighteen men sitting around the table. I had been coming to the meetings above the Pilot and Loft lounges for about two months. I saw a notice that said "Men's Step Study Group On Wednesdays at Six P.M." I asked a fella named David to be my sponsor. He thought it would be a good idea for me to join this as we were going round and round, butting heads about God and step three.

I could go with the first step that I was powerless over alcohol, because when I drank, I couldn't stop. The way the thinker in my old noggin worked, and the way the old world was, I could not, not drink. I was still an agnostic but I considered that a bunch of drunks who drank like I did and weren't drinking were a power greater than me. I thought they could restore me to sound thinking — as far as alcohol was concerned — so I had no problem with step two. But step three was like having to cross the Grand Canyon.

I had seen the Holy Spirit take over people and the fanaticism of those who had been born again. My friend B.W. Stevenson had quit drinking, found the Lord, was on the 700 Club and the last time I saw him, was no fun whatsoever. Of course I was drinking and he wasn't.

The Monday before the Wednesday step study, David and I went to Denny's. I told him that if I made a decision to turn my will and life over to the care of God, I could end up a missionary in China.

He tore open a packet of Sweet and Low, poured it in his ice tea, and said, "Ray, I honestly don't think God wants you to represent Him to the Chinese."

That seemed to make a lot of sense. I had a preconceived idea of what would happen if I took this step, but on the way home, I made a decision to work all twelve steps and see what happened.

That study meeting — which Duke chaired — happened to be on the third step. After reading about being convinced that we were alcoholic and could not manage our own lives and that no human power could relieve our alcoholism, and that God could and would if He were sought, all eighteen men got down on our knees and recited the third step prayer. In it, we made a decision to turn our will and our lives over to the care of God.

I wasn't asking this God to boss me around and tell me what to do and I was pretty sure I wasn't going to hear a voice from out of the clouds telling me to raise an army, attack England and restore Charles VII to the throne of France. It seems I had only asked whatever power there was in the universe to guide my actions and my thoughts.

After an uncomfortable silence we rose to our feet and all of us just kind of stood there and then Duke said, "Ray, you want to close the meeting with the serenity prayer and not the short version?" We all stood up and grasped hands.

"God grant me the serenity to accept the things I cannot change, the courage to change the things I can, and the wisdom to know the difference."

The guys said, "Keep coming back, it works if you work it." The meeting was over.

Duke and I walked outside.

"You really going to Mexico?"

"I got no choice, brother. I got caught red handed selling to an undercover DEA. I'm toast; third time. I'll be okay. Better than five to ten. 'Course the only Spanish I know is kilo, so it'll be funky."

"Well man, if I can do anything, let me know. By the way, what did you mean not the short version? What's the short version of the serenity prayer?"

"God grant me the serenity to…aw, fuck it..."

*FTDD = Full Time Dope Dealer

The Knives of Spain

Written by Ray Wylie Hubbard
Snake Farm Publishing (SESAC)

If I had some poet's wings I would fly to New Orleans
I'd rhyme my trials and my misdeeds
So if you cut the words they would bleed
And in the night when I'm all alone
And the sadness goes to the bone
I'd make the words in the refrain
As lethal as the knives of Spain

If I had some black cat's bones
I'd take the things down to Antone's
Then I'd steal what I really need
I'd take it home and I'd let it bleed
And in the night when I'm by myself
I'd take what it was down from the shelf
When I find the words in the refrain
As lethal as the knives of Spain

If I had some grains of faith
Well I'd keep 'em where they were safe
Then I would not disbelieve
Be corrupted or deceived
And in the night when no one's around
I would kneel down upon the ground
When I find the words in the refrain
As lethal as the knives of Spain

rwh

before you co-write with anybody first make known your intent by insisting it is to be split publishing with whoever you are writing with at that time only.
i wrote a song with this cat, just the two of us, and then on his record i look and there was another writer on it.
i called the dude and asked what was that about. he said, well in the studio the producer wanted to change a couple of the words so he put himself on as a writer and took 1/3 of the writer's credit and publishing.
we would have lawyered up but he was a good kid.
we bit on a bullet and let it go.
it's oily but it's the way it is when people realize there's money to be made off songwriting.
the record sold a few copies.
now here's something else.
don't sign a publishing deal unless you get something in return of value.
there is this idea of "doing something on spec," which the idea is do something now (like sign away your publishing) expecting great returns in the future.
what that really means is "spec to not get paid."
be careful out there.

chapter 16

Lingerie Shows, Finger Picking Lessons

David starts dating a girl that I used to date so he thinks I should get a new sponsor because it might get awkward. I find this old armed robber who moved to Dallas from Oklahoma who smokes Tareytons with a hook. He told me he lost his right hand while drunk, but he never told me how, just that he put it where he shouldn't have.

My career as a musician and songwriter was ... well I didn't have one. An example of a gig at this time was me playing Friday nights at Charlie's Lounge on Mockingbird Lane near Love Field airport doing three 45-minute sets. In between sets there was a lingerie show with some women that you did not want to see in a negligee if you were sober.

So Charles and I are driving to a Salvation Army in Fort Worth to speak and I told him of my frustration at being 42 and just spinning my wheels, and how all I did for my 20s and 30s as far as a music career was concerned was drink beer and J.T.S. Brown whiskey, do dope, throw up a lot and pee. I just never could get through the gates into being a legitimate artist or whatever, and now it was getting kind of scary to be doing what I was at my age.

Charles asked, "Well, what do you want to be?"

I said, "a real songwriter."

He said, "Well write some real songs."

I said, "I can't write the kind of songs I want to cause I can't play guitar good enough."

He answered, "Take some guitar lessons."

I said I couldn't do that.

"Why not?" he asked.

"I would be embarrassed," I replied

"Would that be fear of embarrassment?" he asked.

I said, "I don't know, I guess."

He put a Tareyton in his lips with his hook, lit it with his good hand and said, "Well, ask God to remove your fear. There is a power in the universe that honors our faith in it. We come to believe in this power and it will do certain things for us. We ask it to remove our fear and if we are still afraid then we act as if our fear has been removed and do it anyway. God won't dial the phone for you."

I had seen this guy play acoustic guitar in the corner of a Pullman train car at the railroad museum in Dallas for a private birthday party for Judy's boss. It was pretty much background cocktail smooth jazzy stuff but at one point he played "Deep River Blues" by Doc Watson and just nailed it. Judy got his phone number from her boss' secretary and the next day I got down on my knees and asked God to remove my fear. Even though I was really embarrassed, I dialed the number.

Okay, at this point I feel I should explain the getting on my knees and praying thing.

Back in December I came into a meeting one night and Doc was at the door and asked me how my praying was going. I said "okay I guess," since I hadn't had a drink in two months or so.

He said when I do the third step prayer I should do it on my knees cause that's the way the old timers did it.

I said, "I don't think I'll do it that way since I still got some issues with the God as we understand him bit and it would bother me to get on my knees and..."

He interrupted me and said, "you didn't seem to have any problems being on your knees throwing up in a commode or being on your knees looking for cocaine in the carpet, now did you? So you tell me you got a problem getting on your knees and asking some creative power underlying the very existence of the universe to care for your life. You did so well on your own that you ended up in Alcoholics Anonymous, buddy roe."

I said, "Since you put it that way, I guess not."

The guitar player's name was Sam Swank. When I asked him if he would teach me to fingerpick, he told me to come on over. I went over to his house and showed him this half-assed, not very clean, picking roll thing I do.

He said, "Well, let's start by putting your fingers where they're supposed to be and when they're supposed to be there."

After about an hour he hands me a piece of paper with a pattern on it and says, "Practice this as if your life depends on it." He paused a moment and then added, "Because if you think about it, it really does."

As I walked out the door, I saw a copy of Alcoholics Anonymous on his kitchen counter.

The Real Trick

Written by Ray Wylie Hubbard
Snake Farm Publishing (SESAC)

Christopher turned 16 on a chemical dependency wing
And on family week his momma come up and she says "I ain't gonna stay for this whole thing "
She says, "I've got more important things to do than to listen to this ungrateful son"
Chris said, "If being a parent's so tough how come just anybody can be one?"

Sweet Melissa she turned her first trick at 17
For some backstreet passes and some hashish in the back of a limousine
Now she's seen it all and she don't want to be here or even anywhere
And at 22 she's got what the boys at the VA call the 1000 yard stare

Ah but the real trick is to find a reason to believe in spite of all this
And the big secret is what you're looking for, you're looking with

Miss Helen Petty she lost her husband of 42 years
Now she don't know what to do with herself
And she just can't seem to stop the tears
And she can't sleep at night and she is so afraid and so alone
There are these bastards who take advantage of these precious desperate souls

Like there is this man on Sunday morning on TV who jumps around and screams and shouts
And he says to get me into Heaven is the only thing that he is about

But to get there I've got to believe what he believes
Well if that's the case I believe I'll take my chances when it's time for me to leave

We are all lengthening shadows cast by a sinking sun
So we need to find this reason to believe in something or someone
But it is hard to believe with just faith alone
We feel betrayed by life when the infidelity is our own

I don't concern my self with how Jesus was born or if he was raised from the dead
It just comes down to the things that he said
So many more than Judas have betrayed his name
And this beautiful ancient wisdom has been prostituted for personal gain

chapter 17

The Black Box, Certain Steps, Judy

I spent a week making a list of all the sons of bitches who had done me wrong. It was a long list, but in order to get to the twelfth step, you've got to do the fourth, which means I need to be free of resentments and the way the book says to do it is to list them, write what they did, see how the resentment effects me and then forgive them. Whoa. That doesn't seem right. I would usually polish a grudge until it shined. Most of my twenties and thirties I spent drinking and plotting revenge.

When I came into the rooms of AA, my life was like a plane crash. There was wreckage and debris everywhere. All I had left was the black box, the tape of the flight running over and over in my head. Some of the my resentments were so bad that the only way I could deal with them was to drink.

So what was happening by writing them down and looking at them was that I got them out of my head. On paper they began to lose power. Instead of being dominated by my negative thoughts, I began to use my thinking to improve my life. I think it was James Allen who compared the mind to a garden. We remove the weeds, which are resentment, doubt and fear, and then good stuff like creativity and inspiration can grow.

So I listed them, saw my part, how it effected me even now thinking about them, and then asked God to help me forgive them. Damn.

Then I listed my fears and asked God to remove them.

So then I listed all I had hurt with my sexual conduct and asked God to show me the right way from here on out. Whoa once again, buddy roe.

God doesn't belong in my sex life I told David. God's over there somewhere and sex is in the back seat of a Chevy behind a nightclub. I just didn't think I could do this prayer at all.

I showed up the next Wednesday and walked into the step study room and Duke was sitting at the head of the table.

"Duke, what happened? You're supposed to be in Mexico or jail."

He smiled and said, "Well, I got to thinking, did I or did I not get down on my knees and turn my will and life over to the care of God with seventeen other men in this room with George Jones singing 'Bartender Blues' from the jukebox in the Pilot Lounge downstairs coming through the floor? It seems I did. Then it occurred to me that God either is or He isn't, so I went to the courthouse, said the long version of the serenity prayer, walked in, surprising even my lawyer that I showed up and the judge gave me five years probation, shocking my lawyer even more. And boys, here I am, a miracle child! What to you say? Let's do the fourth step."

I went home and said the prayer asking God to guide me in questionable sex situations, but I didn't really mean it.

Then I did the fifth step like the book said, with an understanding person, and I got some relief from the past; and then went on to steps six and seven. I would add that entirely ready means pretty fucking ready.

So then I made a list of all the people I had harmed and it was pretty long.

I was dragging my feet and not moving forward with the ninth step in making direct amends to these people I wronged. Every one in the step group was waffling too.

So I was at the Phoenix Group Tuesday night with Doc and Duke and this kid named Bobby who was in the step group and had about four months sober. You would think that with that much time without drinking or drugging he wouldn't show up with a fresh bullet hole in his truck that night, but you'd be wrong.

We were setting on the row of chairs against the back wall and this woman walks by...scratch that. The word is *sashays* by, in this tight expensive Sacs Fifth Avenue dress.

She is walking in what is an obvious stripper's gait to the rhythm of a low down Jimmy Reed song playing in her head and as she goes by, I said, "Need some help with that?"

She heard me but just kept on walking.

After the meeting I was standing by the coffee machine with

Doc and she walks up and he says, "Judy, this is Ray. Ray, this is Judy."

She said, "I've seen you before. Aren't you Ray Wylie Hubbard?"

"Yeah."

She asked, "So if I married you, would I be Judy Wylie Hubbard?"

"In order for that to happen, I would have to try you out first. And if you passed certain criteria and we should get married and then we had a kid, you would be known as Mother Hubbard. And if that wasn't bad enough, in certain circles and possibly the media, you would be referred to as the 'Redneck Mother' for the rest of your life."

She didn't say anything for a moment, then turned around and walked off.

Doc said, "She drives a Lincoln, has insurance, cable TV and is eight years sober. You blew it, my man."

Without Love
(We're Just Wasting Time)

Written by Ray Wylie Hubbard
Snake Farm Publishing (SESAC)

You are like a flower growing in the wild wood
Bringing pleasure to the eyes
I am like a river after a rainstorm
Ragin' away too fast to die
You are a flower, I am a river
Without love we're just wastin' time

You are a rainbow spread against a blue sky
The sunrise is your next of kin
I am like a whirlwind roaring across the desert
The kind some hope to never see again
You are a rainbow, I am a whirlwind
Without love we're just wastin' time

You are like a diamond shining in the sunlight
Sparklin' and precious to see
I am like a drifter always going some place
I never get to where I'm supposed to be
You are a diamond I am a drifter
Without love we're just wastin' time

You are like a prayer rising up to Heaven
Pleasing the one upon who you call
I am like a scarecrow alone in the distance
There are those who would see me fall
You are a prayer, I am a scarecrow
Without love we're just wastin' time

chapter 18

Dead Plants, Amends, Wrestling, Rusty

I was going to these meetings and I seemed to catch myself staring at this Judy and then I caught her looking at me.

She came up to me one night and asked, "How much time you got?"

I told her I had six months.

She said, "Damn, they're going to say you can't get in a relationship or even date for a year."

I replied, "I don't date.

"You want your car door opened or a candle light dinner with some flowers, you get yourself a guy with collared shirts. You want to see me, come to the gig, pay the cover and we'll see what happens after the club closes."

Obviously no one has talked to her like this and I knew I had her interest.

The next night after the meeting for some reason, Judy, Duke and I all got in Judy's Lincoln and went to see the movie *Bull Durham*. We got back to the parking lot where we left our vehicles and after Duke left, Judy and I sat in her car and talked for a while. After about an hour, I tell her I'd better leave. There was a long quiet moment and then we kissed. I got home and called my sponsor to tell him I think I should ask this Judy out.

He said, "How can you expect to have a relationship with a woman when you can't even keep a plant alive?"

He hasn't ever been to my house so how did he know?

We went to dinner with Judy and her sponsor and it was decided we could go out on a date when I finished the ninth step.

That Wednesday I got my list and got to it: Everybody on it. I called people, drove over to see them and told them I was wrong for what I did and asked what could I do to make it right. Club owners, music stores, guitar makers, the Buck and Ruck liquor store, next door neighbors, band mates, ex-wife, son, in-laws, a gambler, a photographer, a soundman, two old girlfriends, three ex-managers, two booking agents, a drug dealer in Fort Worth and a partridge in a pear tree. Just kidding, I never harmed a partridge.

It was intense but I did it.

I got up Friday morning and drove three hours to the Hugo, Oklahoma cemetery. I stood over my mother and father's graves and said I was wrong for what I did. Since they couldn't tell me how to make it right, I could only assume they would want me not to drink and be good.

I drove the eleven miles to Soper, Oklahoma, and parked in front of the small white wooden church that my grandmother had taken me to when I was a kid. I set in my truck for a moment and then I got out and walked inside. There was no one there.

I got on my knees and said, "God, I was wrong not to believe in you, and to doubt your existence and to use you in cuss words."

There is only one name left on the list.

I got back to Dallas about five and went over to Pat Toomay's house to make my last amend. I asked him if I could use his phone and he says sure. I called Judy from his house and hand the phone to Pat.

He says, "He's done. He'll pick you up at eight."

She says, "Tell him I'm ready…I mean, I'll be ready."

I got about two blocks from my house and my truck quits and won't start. I walked home and called my ex-mother in law Jerry Crawford and said, "I have a date. Can I borrow your truck?"

"You bet," she answered.

I showered and got dressed and she came to pick me up in her old orange and black and white Dodge pickup that she uses at her house in Seagoville to haul trash in. I dropped her off at her penthouse on Turtle Creek and I was on my way to pick up Judy when I realized that I didn't have any money whatsoever. No credit card, no checkbook, no ATM, not a fucking cent.

I got to Judy's house, honk and she came running out and got in this three-tone, orange and white and black work truck and asks where we're going.

I told her, "I'm gonna surprise you."

We drove down to the Sportatorium for Friday night wrestling. Since I know the Von Erichs, Gentleman Chris Adams and Michael Hayes, Bam Bam and the Freebirds, Judy and I went through the wrestlers entrance, walked through the dressing rooms and they all said hi. I introduced Judy to them and we got our passes and set down to watch the matches.

After the Freebirds beat the Von Erichs for the Texas Tag Team Heavyweight belt, we went back into the dressing room for our goodbyes and I asked Judy if she was hungry and wanted something to eat.

She said she was, so we went over to the Longhorn Ballroom further down on Industrial Boulevard where Rusty Weir was performing. I went to the backstage door, told them who I was and they let us in. We went to Rusty's dressing room and met him and his band.

I took Judy over to his deli trey full of cheese and vegetables and meats and said, "help yourself." I picked up some crackers and Monterrey jack cheese and put them on a paper plate.

We watched Rusty do his set, I went out and sang "Don't It Make You Want To Dance," with him, and then we went back to Judy's house.

I walked her up to the door and we kiss for like a minute. Then I went home and called her and we talked on the phone till the sun was coming up.

I said, "Well, the farm report is coming on TV so I guess we better hang up. I'll see you at Phoenix tonight."

Only later did she realize that I hadn't spent a cent on her.

The next night she invited me to her house for dinner and after we eat, we are sitting in her living room and drinking coffee.

The next thing we know it's about two o'clock in the morning.

I said, "I guess I better be going."

She answered, "Why don't you spend the night"

I asked, "Where would I sleep?"

She picked up the coffee cups, walked to the kitchen, and said, "Don't be an idiot."

She went into the bedroom while I went to the bathroom. I started sweating realizing I hadn't had sex sober since...since...I think ever. There was always at least a six-pack involved since high school...maybe there were times, but at that moment I didn't remember them. As I was standing there in her bathroom, I recalled myself thinking of the last part of the fourth step about remembering what I said about God doesn't belong in my sex life. Well, I changed my mind. If I ever meant a prayer more sincerely than when I prayed for my testicles to drop when I was thirteen, I don't remember it. I closed my eyes and said out loud, "God, just let the thing work."

It did.

Preacher

Written by Ray Wylie Hubbard
Snake Farm Publishing (SESAC)

Preacher come by today, preacher come by today
He talked a whole lot but didn't have much to say

Told me of a place with streets of gold
Told me of a place with streets of gold
He went on to say that God and the devil both want my soul

Said my life was empty, something was missing
Said my life was empty, something was missing
Carried on and on about how his Savior lived in the world above this one

My woman she was hanging clothes on the line
My woman she was hanging clothes on the line
I said "Look out yonder preacher
Now tell me have you ever seen anything as fine?

See how she moves slow, see how she moves slow
You can see I ain't missing nothing when she stoop down low."

Preacher closed his Bible and he put his hat on his head
He closed his Bible and he put his hat on his head
He took off down the road, must have been something I said.

chapter 19

Being Even, Seeing Stevie Again

Now I had been going to like a meeting a day for eight or nine months, I had admitted I was powerless over alcohol; I came to believe; begrudgingly turned my will and my life over to the care of God; did an inventory; told someone about it; looked at my shortcomings; asked God to remove them; listed the people I hurt and made amends to them all. I had done all that. You would think that by doing all that I would be ahead of the game.

Well, I am not ahead, I am just even. Even. Even with the past; for me this is a great place to be, probably for anybody really.

So I was now into step ten. Which means if I do something wrong I have to make an amends and if somebody wrongs me, I've got to forgive them. Doesn't seem fair but I didn't write the book.

Trying to meditate showed me how undisciplined my thinking really was. But I was seeing the benefits of acting my way into right thinking.

I have had a spiritual awakening as the result of doing the twelve steps the way the book said to do them.

A spiritual awakening is kind of hard to explain. It would probably involve some calculus and charts and calculators and other cerebral stuff and I don't want to show off, so let's just say I had one.

But I still cussed and smoked cigarettes.

I still have a ways to go before my canonization (I don't know what that means but Thom thinks I should leave it in).

Now this sounds like I made it up but it is the gospel truth. I have witnesses.

I got my one year chip at the Phoenix group. After the meeting Judy, Doc, Duke, Bobby and about twenty of us went to a Mexican restaurant on Loop 12, and were sitting there eating when Stevie Ray walked in with his mother. I got up and went over to his table and showed him my chip. I thanked him for talking the time to talk to me a year ago last November. He introduced me to his mother and asked, "You got a sponsor and working the steps?"

I told him, "Yeah, I finished my ninth and am doing ten and eleven and twelve daily."

He smiled and hugged me and said "There ain't no elevators, brother, you got to take the steps."

That was the last thing he said to me and it's the first thing I say to kids who ask me to sponsor them.

There are Some Days

Written by Ray Wylie Hubbard
Snake Farm Publishing (SESAC)

Well I seem to be haunted by these ghosts
I can't decide which ones grieve me most
Not wanting to remember or I can't forget
I am dusty with old regrets

There are some days I just wanna cry
There are some ways I use to get by

Well you got your cross and your hymnal too
And you say you're prayers like you're supposed to do
And you say it was amazing grace
Well I believe you, I see it in your face

Now I have seen this angel and her wings are torn
She offers me a string of pearls and thorns
She seems to smile before she disappears
She whispers, "You're not the only one bleeding here."

rwh

I was playing at whole foods in dallas for a radio station food bank fundraiser and was having a big poker party that night with duke and bobby and a bunch of guys from the phoenix group and judy and some girls were going to be there too. I was falling for her and as I finished my gig I noticed a face painting booth set up for kids. I walked over. That night as the cards were dealt around the table I kept making eye contact with judy standing over by the door. We were playing the last hand after about three or four hours and I figured it was time. As I shuffled the cards I saw judy looking at me. I set the cards down on the table and took off my denim jacket and nonchalantly rolled up the sleeve of my t shirt revealing a red heart on my arm with the name judy written in black cursive in it with an arrow stuck through it. I picked up the cards and shuffled and dealt them around the table. The guys whooped and hollered and judy blushed and I think it was duke who sang "tonight's the night" by neil young and I knew I was going to ask her to marry me.

Just to Hold You

Written by Ray Wylie Hubbard
Snake Farm Publishing (SESAC)

All you know of me is my reputation
Some have called me a storm about to rage
But if you'll take me and not forsake me
I'll give to you my heart in a golden cage
For I love you with reckless abandon
And I've loved you like that from the start
It's my good fortune just to know you
Your eyes put wildness in my heart

Down from the mountains I come like thunder
For I've lain too long where the cold rivers run
Just to know you just to flow with you
Just to grow with you and to reap and sow with you
Just to hold you when you when your hair's undone

Like a flash of lightning in the heavens
Some lives light up a darkened sky
There are others who fall and stumble
They'll hide their hearts and their love deny
But if you'll take me and not forsake me
If you'll have me just as I am
I will love you beyond forever
And I'll pledge to you my heart upon sacred ground

Out in the badlands they call me an outlaw
But I'll stand on the words of St. Paul
Though we speak like angels and gain the whole world
But don't have love, we have nothing at all
But if I displease you and you don't want me
Well I still wish you love for love is blessed
We can take nothing greater upon our journey
Rest assured we need take nothing less

chapter 20

Marriage, Fertility, Louie

"Sorry guys. I got to take a break from recording here and get back home for about an hour. I'll be back in a little bit."

Terry Ware said, "We're in the middle of laying down tracks. What's so important?"

So I told him.

"I got to go home and do some of that damned old sex."

Judy and I were trying to get pregnant and we had gone and done the fertility stuff the doctor ordered. When the ovaries stirred and said it was time, it was time, no matter what, for my unit and testicles to show up and do their job.

Oh yeah, Judy and I had gotten married. I quit smoking exactly one month before the wedding so I was a little puffy from sucking on lemon drops for 30 days.

She was working at Bankston Lincoln Mercury heading up the leasing department and I was taking guitar lessons from Sam Swank and doing some gigs with Terry Ware, Ron Thompson and Guthrie Kennard.

I heard vinyl was dying and compact disc was the wave of the future so I borrowed some money from Judy's dad and went into the studio in Garland, Texas, where Willie cut *Red Headed Stranger*. I was recording the first songs I wrote sober. Since I had no idea how to get a record deal, I figured I'd do it myself, and put it out and let people know that I wasn't dead or drunk or dead drunk.

At the studio I picked up a flyer for a pressing company in Nashville that does everything. You send them the master and the artwork, and five weeks later you've got a thousand CDs. So I called them and talked to Louie who runs the place. He sent me a sample of their work for bluegrass and country-gospel albums. They sound good, so he's the guy.

We decided to go to Masterphonics in Nashville on 17th Avenue to master it. After it was done, we walked over to Louie's on 16th to hand deliver it. I called and made an appointment. It was a struggle but I was really satisfied with the songs, the music, the production and the artwork. After all the dead ends, underfunded projects and just fucked-up attempts in the past to make records and the frustrations of failing time after time, I felt that this was it. So after twenty years of heartbreak, this was my time.

Terry Ware and I walked into Louie's office with the master and the artwork.

Louie was dressed in ostrich skin cowboy boots, starched Levi jeans, a belt with a big buckle, an expensive western shirt and aviator sunglasses.

He stood up from behind his desk and stuck out his hand and said, "Ray, so glad to meet you. I think you'll be really satisfied with the quality of our work here and you're just gonna love the final results. We really appreciate your business."

I shook his and hand and he paused for a moment then asked, "Is someone with you?"

I smiled and said, "Yeah, my guitar player Terry here. What's the matter? You blind?"

He stuck his hand into the air about five feet from where Terry was standing and answered, "As a matter of fact, I am."

He sat down and said, "Let me get some information from you," and begins typing on what I assume is a braille typewriter.

I looked at Terry. We sat down and I answered Louie's questions almost by rote. I seemed to be having an out-of-body experience.

"I am giving my artwork to a blind guy. I am really giving my artwork to a guy who can't see. The music I can understand but the artwork? God, is this some kind of joke? You think this is funny? I quit drinking and turn my will and life over to your care and this is the result? Louie is blind, God, in case you didn't know. I mean, really. I don't expect much, just an even playing field, maybe. But this? I mean even Columbus had a compass. His navigator probably wasn't blind. Custer at least had some guns. They had a chance. Don't you have to see art to appreciate it or to even work with it?"

I left my master and the camera-ready artwork for my cover with Louie and walked out in a haze, not believing what just happened.

We drove back to Dallas hardly saying a word.

Somewhere near Texarkana, Terry said, "You know, for a blind guy, he dressed pretty sharp."

Wanna Rock n Roll

Written by Ray Wylie Hubbard
Snake Farm Publishing (SESAC)

Last night I went down to the railroad tracks to watch that train roll by
99 cars screaming into the dark I heard the lonesome whistle cry
With her name on my arm and the rain coming down I kissed her like the first time
I took her down to the railroad tracks and her red, red lips touched mine

She said,"I wanna rock and roll
Wanna hoochie coo
Shake that thing
Baby, love me do"

The woman's got a walk to make a man cry, throw back his head and howl
Ruby red lips, liquid hips, more than the law will allow
If I told her once, I told her twice I must have told her a thousand times
I got a red hot mind and a cold black heart, I am the jealous kind
The woman just laughed and said, "Sweet Daddy, you know you're the only one
You're my smooth lover boy, my heartache and joy, come on let's have some fun"

It was early last night, I went downtown to a place called Johnny's Last Stand
Through the blues and the smoke I saw her on the dance floor she's with another man
The dead man's name was Louie Dupree I pushed the little button on my knife
I walked up and said, "Hello boys and girls have you enjoyed your life?"

Last night I went down to the railroad tracks to watch that train roll by
99 cars screaming into the dark, I heard the lonesome whistle cry
With her name on my arm and the rain coming down, I kissed her for the very last time
I took her down to the railroad track and her red, dead lips touched mine

rwh

(this is another version of a conversation I think is important so look at it as a déjà vu if you already read it or a flash forward if it comes up later)
so what do you want to do charles asks.
i say well i wanna be a songwriter.
well then write some songs.
i can't.
why not he asks?
well i don't know how to play guitar good enough.
well take lessons he says.
i can't do that, i would be embarrassed…i mean i'm ray wylie hubbard and i'm 42 years old and to take my acoustic guitar to a music store with these kids with blue mohawks and guitars shaped like spaceships…man how uncool would that be?
well wouldn't you say that would be the fear of being embarrassed?
well yeah, i guess.
you believe in God by now don't you?
yeah.
well, ask God to remove your fear and act as if your fear were removed. God ain't gonna dial the phone for you.
so i called sam swank.
now here i am 42, sober a year, met judy, we're dating and i got nothing going on as far as a career at all. i'm still gigging at charlie's airport lounge between the underwear sales girls sets.
charles calls me and says i have volunteered you to give a step talk at an aa group in tyler and i'll pick you up but bring a notebook and a pen.
we start driving and he says open your notebook and write 'goals' at the top of the page.
i say what do you mean?
he says what do you want in your life. what is your goal? you didn't sober up just to go to meetings.
i say well i wanna be a songwriter.
he says write it down. but what kind of songwriter do you want to be?
i said a good one.
he said how about a prosperous, award winning songwriter. might as well set high goals cause if you set low goals, you deny what you can be with God's help.
i said sure.

okay now on the left side of the page write down 'the things i got going for me.'
like what?
1. you're sober
2. you ain't burned all your bridges...least not the one you sleeping under.
3. you have a personality that's not offensive right off...i don't know...just think of things that are in your favor.
4. you have a faith where you had none before
5. you know how to sing in a microphone in front of people...think about it. you don't have to do all this right now.
okay now on the right side at the top write down 'what i need to do to attain this goal of being an award winning prosperous songwriter.'
like what?
like 1. you wanna be a songwriter...better find out about publishing doncha think? study the music business of publishing
2. take guitar lessons
3. record a cd to show people you ain't dead or drunk
4. play in front of a performer's crowd that you want to make your crowd...just give it some time. you don't have to do it right now. you with me so far?
i say yeah.
he says okay now in the center of the page write 'remove fear and doubt.'
whenever you doubt yourself or think your songwriting isn't good, you ask yourself 'where's the proof?' there is no proof except what your head tells you. fear and doubt are the things that limit us...if we remove out fear and doubt...it is unlimited what we may become. got it?
i guess.
jeez. do you believe it?
yes...i do.
now write 'time and effort' in the middle of the page.
i do so.
now at the bottom of the page write 'purpose.'
i did.
now let's say since the beginning of time whether God created the world in six days or there was a big bang and after billions of years a fish flopped out on

land and grew legs and then became a monkey and then a neanderthal and finally a man…whatever, here in the universe we might say a purpose of the universe is to strengthen and ennoble mankind…to inspire whether conscious or not...to better himself… okay, you with me?

i say i am.

well then we gonna make that your purpose…you are going to write songs that contribute to life by giving people joy and inspiring them and make them feel better about themselves and to strengthen and ennoble them and therefore your purpose in being a prosperous songwriter is the same purpose as the universe.

so now if you are putting forth the time and effort to do the right column on a daily basis…and your fear and doubt has been removed and you are in cahoots with the creative intelligence underlying the material world and life as we know it…there is nothing to keep you from attaining your goals, is there? think of anything?

well don't cause it will happen. we just don't know the time frame.

now the deal is and i heard this somewhere, 'the tragedy isn't in not attaining your goals…the tragedy is not having a goal to attain.'

now when you talk tonight…don't embarrass me.

Black Wings

Written by Ray Wylie Hubbard
Snake Farm Publishing (SESAC)

Fly away on them old wings black as they may be
Believing what you leave behind is burnt up and junk debris
And every last undying soul resides at a hotel in Saint Marie
So fly away on them old wings black as they may be

Fly away on them old wings black as they may be
Shimmerin' like a Leslie and a Hammond b3
Or a shaking tambourine at a gospel jubilee
So fly away on them old wings black as they may be

Fly away on them old wings black as they may be
Jangling and jingling all the way to Tennessee
Trusting in a duo jet and a 9 volt battery
So fly away on them old wings black as they may be

Fly away on them old wings black as they may be
Strumming on a Stella guitar and singing 'Deportee'
Now that ain't much of a repertoire, oh no sirree
So fly away on them old wings black as they may be

Fly away on them old wings black as they may be
You'll never gonna reach the sun or the Sunset Marquis
You'll die like a saint on high alongside gamblers and thieves
Fly away on them old wings black as they may be

Mom, dad, me (inside mom)

Me wanting something

Soper, OK house

Adamson Senior picture

Faces West: Wayne Kidd, me, Rick Fowler

Poster for the Outpost

7he Raggedy Sometime Band: me, Jo Wright, Jerry Graves, Larry Groce

The Cowboy Twinkies album

THE OUTPOST

PROFESSIONAL ENTERTAINMENT IN A FRIENDLY ATMOSPHERE

THREE FACES WEST

Will be your host in this high country entertainment mecca THE OUTPOST promises a delightful evening of the finest in professional entertainment and unique atmosphere.

Located directly behind the bank and opening at 5:00 p.m., with three shows nightly, THE OUTPOST will complete your Red River vacation.

During the past year, I've had many opportunities to enjoy the performances of THREE FACES WEST. I've watched them grow into one of the finest groups I've heard. They are a unique group whose talent spans many areas of music: from Blues to Bluegrass; from Folk Ballads to Folk Rock; from Popular to Commercial. It is this ability to please so many tastes that convinces me that we will all be hearing much from them in the near future. In addition to the outstanding variety of instrumental and vocal styles, they put on a fantastic stage show. Their hip humor is quick and that makes for something more than just another singing group. It transforms them from just singers to great entertainers. In simple summation, their ballads are harmonic, their up-tempo numbers—driving, their popular—heavy, their traditional sounds—ethnic, their humor—hilarious. THREE FACES WEST!! They're fantastic!!

Roy Applegate

FOLK MUSIC, U.S.A.

THE OUTPOST
GENERAL DELIVERY
RED RIVER, NEW MEXICO
87558

Me explaing why we didn't get paid
to Terry, Jimmy, Clovis

Paul Pearcy, John Inmon,
me, Bob Livingston

B. W. Stevenson, Rusty Weir,
Steve Fromholz, me

Bugs Henderson and me

Mr. fancy

John Inmon, Gary Macdonald, me, Dan Kinney, Bob Livingston in front of Christine, our bus

Another Loco Gringo

Me with mullet,
Willie with mullet,
Judy with hat

Jerry Jeff Walker and me

Another Willie picnic

Me and Liverpool drummer

Jerry Wexler postcard

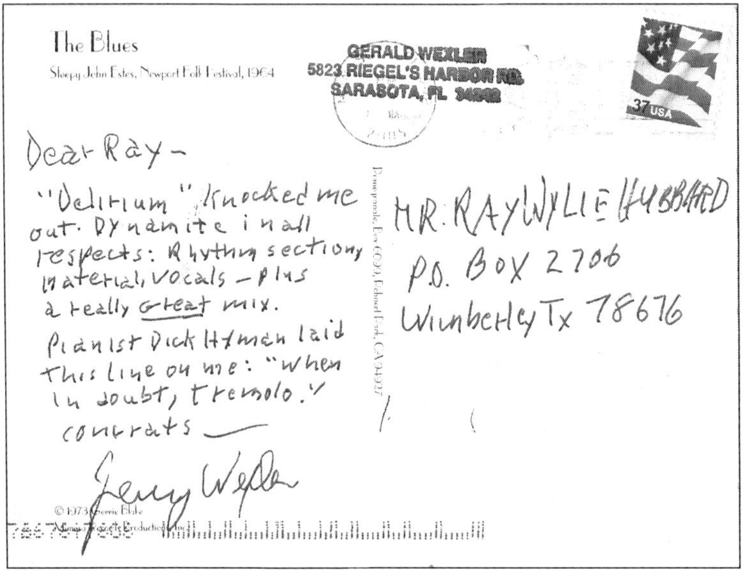

The Blues
Sleepy John Estes, Newport Folk Festival, 1964

GERALD WEXLER
5823 RIEGEL'S HARBOR RD.
SARASOTA, FL

37 USA

Dear Ray –

"Delirium" knocked me out. Dynamite in all respects: Rhythm section, material, vocals – plus a really great mix.

Pianist Dick Hyman laid this line on me: "when in doubt, tremolo."

congrats —

Jerry Wexler

MR. RAY WYLIE HUBBARD
P.O. BOX 2706
Wimberley Tx 78676

© 1973 Gerrie Blake

My Frankenstein guitar

Kyle, John Michael, me and Lucas on the way into Letterman studios

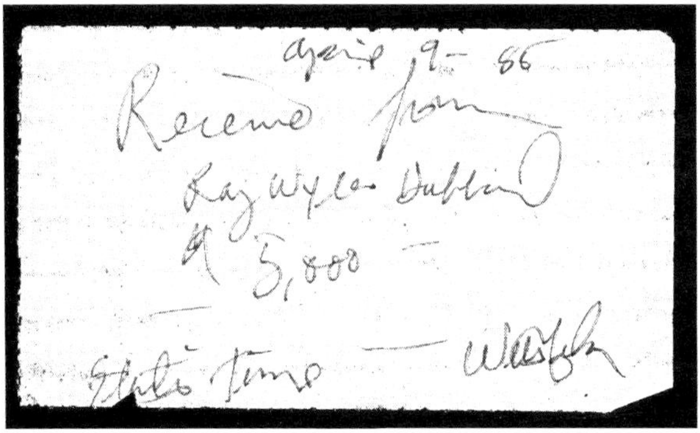

Willie Receipt

My son Cory, me, my son Lucas

Me and Lucas (age 12)

Me and the boy

Lucas, Judy, me, Angel at the homestead

chapter 21

Lucas, "15:21...Okay, 'Cole"

Judy says, "I think my water broke."

I said, "We still got five weeks."

She calls her doctor and he tells us to come on in.

We got to the hospital and they told us they'd induce labor in about five hours and for me to go home and get her overnight stuff.

I went back to the house and the phone rang. It's them telling me I better get back…it's happening.

When I got there, I saw Judy as they were wheeling her in. They told me they were going to prepare her and for me to go to the waiting room — they'll come get me when it's time.

It's a Saturday afternoon and I'm in the waiting room. Any minute Judy is going to give birth. The TV is on to Fort Worth's channel 11 matinee movie. It's a black-and-white western from the '50s, and the Indians are attacking a wagon train. And I swear on the bible, a pioneer woman is giving birth and a cowboy says, "boil some water." Arrows are flying through the air and sticking in wagon wheels. The wagon the woman is under catches fire… then the hospital people came in. They said, "let's go."

The five-and-a-half pound boy came out crying. The doctor cut the cord and showed him to us. We tear up, too.

Judy told me his first name is Lucas, and I can pick his middle name.

I say, "Fifteen Twenty-One…"

"What?"

I repeat, "Fifteen Twenty-One. His name would be 'Luke 15:21.'"

She asks, "What in the hell are you taking about?"

"Luke 15:21 from the New Testament…it's a bible verse…what a great name…'Luke 15:21 Hubbard.'"

She just looked at me.

I shrugged and said, "okay...'Cole.'"

Wild Gods of Mexico

Written by Ray Wylie Hubbard
Snake Farm Publishing (SESAC)

There's a lot I don't understand
There's so much that I don't know
Lately I've been thinking about
The wild gods of Mexico

Mr. Campbell says there's feathered serpents
Highly revered a thousand years ago
Now days nobody much recalls
The wild gods of Mexico

Hearsay's got 'em viscous and vain
Demanding blood and flesh and bones
Sacrifice was what it was
For the wild gods of Mexico

The woman I love desired a child
She abandoned hope as we grew old
In desperation I swore an oath
To the wild gods of Mexico

With conviction and for recompense
I took a dog and I cut its' throat
Drained its blood into a wooden cup
For the wild gods of Mexico

Now there's a lot I don't understand
There's so much that I don't know
Someday soon I'll tell my son
About the wild gods of Mexico

The Last Younger Son

Written by Ray Wylie Hubbard
Snake Farm Publishing (SESAC)

My last name is Younger, I am the last Younger son
The name I was given was Luke 15:21
Three days of thunder three days of rain
I come to be in this world with a number and a name

My last name is Younger, I am the last Younger son
I stand as a witness to the things I have done
I have caused sorrow, yet I too have been pained
You cannot be in this world and not get stained

My last name is Younger, I am the last Younger son
I once had beliefs and now I have none
There's no forgiveness for old guns and knives
Perhaps it is fitting we don't recall our past lives

My last name is Younger, I am the last Younger son
There is a secret I never told anyone
Sometimes I see something in a few certain eyes
And I behold the future of how and when a man dies

My last name is Younger, I am the last Younger son
I won't get no older than the age of 21
As I look in the mirror I see the future once more
An old friend is waiting just beyond the closed door

rwh

so troy campbell calls me like at about 6 in the afternoon. i been sponsoring him for about six months and he was doing the steps. he sounds frantic. i say calm down and tell me what's happening. he races away: man, i'm over here in norway or sweden and i'm at the place i just played and they loved me and it's great over here and townes used to come over here and gram parsons is huge here and i just met these two gorgeous blonde viking women and they want me to go home with them, just me and them and they said they would both do me and they're wildly beautiful and i think they're high but i could probably go with them and not get high and have sex with both of them, i mean i'm pretty sure i could, yeah i could and…not get high, i mean, but i'm kinda concerned a little cause you told me i couldn't get in a relationship till i had a year sober and it's not really a relationship, it's just tonight and i think i will be okay but i wanted to call and just let you know and see if you thought i could or if you thought i shouldn't, i mean two scandinavian women, ray, i think it's God's will, i mean here i am and what do you think? i think i should but i don't wanna do anything to jeopardize my sobriety and… and so what should i do?

i said troy, i'm not your chick sponsor. i'm your aa sponsor and the first year of sobriety is a fragile time so we've got to be careful in putting ourselves in situations where we not only have the opportunity to drink and drug but we've got to remember we are powerless over the first drink unless we maintain a good spiritual condition and…and…ah...there's how many of them? two? viking women? hmmm. well… what i think is you should do is fire me and get a sponsor that would let you fuck 'em.

Last Train to Amsterdam

Written by Ray Wylie Hubbard
Snake Farm Publishing (SESAC)

There's an old soul waiting to be born
There's a scarecrow standing in the corn
One of them is wishing for the light of day
One of them is chasing all the black crows away

Well I'm standing at the station
And I don't know where I am
And the wheels are turning
On the last train to Amsterdam

There's a hobo waiting on a train
There's a hitch hiker standing in the rain
One of them knows he's never going home
The other one feels a little chill down in his bones

There's a preacher out spreading the word
There's a blond in a Thunderbird
One of them tells me to kneel and pray
One of them gets to me in a real bad way

Well I got me a one-way ticket
To get me from where I am
And the wheels are turning
On the last train to Amsterdam

I'm standing a little south of Fate
There ain't no exit from the interstate
There's one way in, it's a long dirty road
There's only one way out, Robert Johnson knows

chapter 22

Poetry, Goats, Loco Gringos, Wimberley

We moved to Poetry, Texas, after we sold the house in Oak Cliff and Carrolton. Poetry, Texas, sounds more romantic than it really is. It sounds like there would be men with ascots drinking brandy, but it was pretty much a bunch of old coot goat farmers.

We got a small house with four acres among these goat farms. The day we were moving in, Judy left work, picked up Lucas at daycare, and then went to our old house to do more packing while I unloaded boxes in Poetry by myself.

About eight that night, a terrible storm came up. It started raining hard and then there was lightning real close with thunder almost at the same time and the house shook and the lights went out.

I looked out my kitchen window above the sink, another flash of lightning lit up the outside, and through the rain I saw the devil walk by.

He was about four feet tall and had horns.

I ducked down on the floor. Then it began to rain harder on our tin roof, tree limbs were blowing against the house and the wind was howling like the doomed souls in Dante's *Inferno*.

I was thinking, "what am I gonna do? I know, I'll get my guitar and sing some old gospel songs, some spirituals, maybe a Baptist hymnal from my childhood."

Then I realized I didn't know any.

A sinking feeling came over me and I just huddled down on the floor in the dark and waited for my demise. The storm passed after about an hour, the moon came through the broken clouds, and everything outside had this spooky, steamy look to it. I looked out my front window and I saw a man in a hat wearing a dark slicker over his overalls walking up my gravel drive way with a chainsaw.

He came up and knocked on the door. I wasn't about to open it. He saw me setting on the floor and opened the door himself. He said his name was Lloyd and that he worked for the

East Texas Electric Company. He told me he had to cut down a tree near my gate that has messed up some telephone wires and my lights should be on in about an hour.

I nodded.

He said, "Welcome to Poetry. We're glad you're here."

I nodded again.

He turned to leave and then turned back around. He said, "You are the whitest guy I've ever seen." I wanted to tell him I had just seen the devil walking around outside in my backyard, but I didn't know if I could talk. I just nodded again.

Only later did someone tell me that goats can walk on their hind legs for about four or five feet learning to balance themselves so they can eat leaves off the lower branches of trees.

Yeah, maybe, but I know what I saw.

While we were in Poetry a record company offered me a deal: They would give me a $15,000-dollar recording budget and they'd spend $15,000 to promote it.

Around the same time, a small independent label called Deja Disc out of San Marcos offered me a deal, too: an $8,000 budget that included recording and promotion.

Easy choice huh? Not so fast honeybunny.

The first offer is from a country label with some old country guys I know that have kind of turned into nostalgia acts.

Deja Disc has Michael Hall, Lisa Mednick, the Coffee Sergeants, Michael Fracasso, and Sarah Elizabeth Campbell. I decided to go with them since I wanted to be associated with a roster of writers like that.

I went into the studio with Lloyd Maines and recorded the album called *Loco Gringo's Lament*. I named the record after a song I wrote about a dreadlocked wildass young hellion in Dallas in the band Loco Gringos who overdosed on heroin. His brother asked me to sing "Redneck Mother" at his wake that was held at Club Dada in Deep Ellum as it was one of the first songs he learned to play on guitar. I did. I have never seen — before or since — people sing that song with tears running down their faces. I was deeply honored.

We recorded the album and were out of money but still had

to mix it and master it. I sold my van and sound system, and Tony Joe White recommended a young engineer named Brian Hardin to mix it.

Loco Gringo's Lament was the first record I ever made that I could hand to someone, look them in the eye and say, "here it is," without wincing or having excuses duct taped to it.

Let me digress here and mention my other — earlier — albums real quick.

After the Cowboy Twinkies Warner/Reprise fiasco, I did the album for Willie with the demos — we know how that went.

Then the *Something About The Night* album was on my own label. My then father-in-law Johnny Crawford put up the money to do that one. Later a promoter/drug dealer walked into his office with $20,000 in cash and leased the rights. We eventually got the rights back when he got busted. Johnny defended him — got him not less than two, nor more than five.

After my divorce, this other drug dealer who was a fan wanted a cassette of me, because he'd put these expensive speakers in his Mercedes. He gave me $1,200. I got a remote truck and recorded a live thing at Soap Creek Saloon with Bugs Henderson, Bobby Chitwood, Ron Thompson and Mandy Mercier. We gave him the cassette and he was happy. Then we pressed up about a thousand copies of *Caught in the Act*. I was dating an exotic dancer who wanted to be a hair stylist. This is why I have a perm in the cover photo.

Do you see a pattern here?

Judy had been working at the car dealership, getting up at six thirty and driving an hour to an hour-and-a-half, just to get to work for the two years we were living in Poetry. She called me one morning and asked me what we would do if she quit her job?

I told her we'd move to Wimberley.

She said, "I'm quitting my job. Go find us a house."

I did, and we moved thirty-eight miles south of Austin.

Loose

Written by Ray Wylie Hubbard
Snake Farm Publishing (SESAC)

I went to see her laid out to meet her saints
She was dressed in white low cut silk and lace
Even her mama said she was always trouble
Promise a man everything, give him half and charge him double

We all gonna bust loose one of these days
We all got to stay loose come what may
We all wanna cut loose on payday
Now we ain't ever gonna break loose of these old rock and roll ways

Now that girl walked like she owned Bourbon Street
And in those days she had grown men kneeling at her feet
She took to an old profession as source of revenue
Now all she's taking with her is a dress from Saks 5th Avenue

She called me up one time and said, "Let's go get tattoos"
I said, "Well let me brush my teeth and find my shoes"
She come down the street in a stolen Volkswagon
She smiled and said she'd decided on a crimson Chinese dragon

Loco Gringo's Lament

Written by Ray Wylie Hubbard
Snake Farm Publishing (SESAC)

A wild young cowboy out on the highway
A Telecaster kid of the rockin' trade
Lost unto the straight and narrow
To honky tonks and masquerades
Tempted by a thousand pleasures
It's foolish comfort for the soul
A deadly shot in the mist of shadows
There ain't no sign posts along this road

It is such a sweet temptation
It gives such a brief relief
It is such a false sensation
How come that's so hard to believe?

Hiram Williams was in the back seat
Of a Cadillac on New Year's Day
He closed his eyes and sang his last song
Mister Leon Payne's "The Lost Highway"
That same old song with the sad sweet ending
Is playing somewhere south of town
By a band of hard young rockers
Who never think they'll see the sun go down

A young angel sings in sorrow
For the broken hearted and betrayed
A last waltz for the wild young cowboy
Who never came back from the lost highway
An old Diablo waits in silence
For the loco gringo young in years
He waits alone in Heaven's shadows
With a stolen horse and tequila tears

rwh

here's ah another songwriting hint...wait...forget it...everybody knows how to write songs. seems what everybody wants to know is how to get them recorded by famous hot shot singers so they can make a ton of money off royalties...well, i can't help you there...in my case, it's been like shooting dice. i've rolled a seven probably four times in my life as far as having one of my songs recorded where it made a little dough after years of shooting snake eyes on the other people recording my songs crap table. but the thing is i never wrote songs with the intended purpose of having anybody else record them. i wrote them because i had no choice. i wrote them not thinking about what was going to happen to them in the future. i just wrote them.

one time waylon jennings asked me to write him some songs.

i said "what kind of songs?"

he said "waylon 'goddam' jennings songs. what else, hoss?" i regret to this day i was unable to empathize in order to do that. now i've heard some cats say that as far as songwriting as a full time getting cuts, collecting royalties occupation goes, that you should go to nashville cause "you must be present to win." that's good advice i would imagine if you wanna do that. i don't. i have a lot of respect for some friends of mine that do that but it ain't for me. i dig where i am, just rolling them bones and when the song is finished i get to sing it for people who come to hear me sing it. oh yeah. after i finish a song...i sing it, then i sing it again and then i say, "thanks." i don't know who or what i'm thanking but i do want to keep that who or what happy so the door stays open for another song to come through. weird, huh? i don't care if it is...been doing it for a while and it's been working for a while.

really? big talk, ray. but what i really wanna know is this: i've written these songs. i got a family so i can't start a band and then get in a van and travel around and play bars and can't get a gig anyway since i don't have a cd being played anywhere. i'd really like to have someone hear them. i can't move to nashville. so what do i do? right now would be a good time to write the word, 'alas.' so…alas. but here goes nothing. some things to remember:

1. there is a fine line that does not need to be crossed as far as getting your songs heard and that line is the difference between being persistent and being a pest.

2. however, it's okay to promote yourself…just don't let anybody see you do it on purpose. now the music business is changing faster than i can keep up with it and i really am more on the fringe of it as in the past on my income tax form there have been years i have been barely above 'hobby status.'

hey ray, i forgot…i don't have any money to go in a studio, hire musicians, record an album, mix it, master it, press it up, hire a radio promoter, hire a publicist... alas. oh alas. okay. here's the deal then. do a youtube thing. wanna get your songs heard? might as well have them seen. as an example. i did my "coricidin bottle" and "south of the river" videos for the total price of 9 bucks for the monkey and 2 dollars for the double a batteries. hang on, i'm gonna go see how many views they got. "coricidin bottle"…13, 262 views…well, 13, 263 since i watched it again. "south of the river"…12, 816. so there you go...bunch of people saw 'em. i don't know if any of the people who saw them bought the cd or even downloaded it but that's not why i did 'em. just wanted to see if i could. and over 10,000 people saw each one so that's pretty amazing for the cost of 11 bucks. see i knew i wasn't going to be on cmt or gac or on television…i figured they were only gonna be seen on a phone or a computer so it didn't have to be shot on 35mm film. so i just did it on my phone. so there you go…i did 'em with imovie and an 8mm app, and most of the time i did something, then pushed a button, said 'rats,' pushed undo, and then tried it again. so do you a video of one of your songs…but hey, don't post 'em on my Facebook page. see # 1 above…just tell me you did one and i'll go to youtube and watch it. or at least 30 seconds of it…i have a short attention span so keep it interesting…no tailgate parties in a country field, no trucks, no dirt roads, no girls in cut offs and boots, no aviator sunglasses, no backward ball caps... it is okay to use a mechanical monkey.

that's great advice, ray. you a most brilliant cat.

you think that's brilliant? how 'bout this? if you're a young broke songwriter and don't have any money to get a good guitar, here's what you do...go to your girlfriend's dad and say if you buy me a gibson j45, you will never see me again.

what?

wow. that's cold, ray. i can't believe you'd say that.

wait, think about it. your girlfriend will have a broken heart for a while, but she'll find someone obviously better for her than you and, you may miss her for a while, but you'll have a gibson j45 and in the long run, you're better off with the blues and having a good guitar to play 'em on. it's worth a few tears.

Coricidin Bottle

Written by Ray Wylie Hubbard
Snake Farm Publishing (SESAC)

Said my prayers to the old black gods
Tied a string around some chicken bones
Set 'em on fire and crossed my heart
Tuned up the Kay and the Silvertone

Rubbed my hands cross the Tolex scars
Took the laces out of my tennis shoes
Now I can live with a 60-cycle hum
Is anybody here got a 50 watt fuse?

Laid down a groove like a monkey gettin' off
Stompin' on the kick, pounding on the tom
If you ever get to heaven say "whew thank you"
If you ever get scared say the 23rd Psalm

I got a Coricidin bottle that I use as slide
And a woman sweet as a tootsie roll
When she kissing and licking and cussing and a grindin'
Shakes the mortal coil round my amaranthine soul

chapter 23

Tic Douloureux, Jeep Flip, Hip by Dr. J.

So one day after about eight months of not drinking...wham! I got a pain on the left side of my face that was like lightning striking the side of my head. It lasted about five minutes. It stopped me dead in my tracks. Then, for the next week it would happen at random.

When it hit, everything stopped. I couldn't move or do anything except try not to move. I'd wanna jump out of my skin just to get away from it. Then it would gradually ease up. It was like having liquid hot molten lead poured on your cheekbone.

I went to a clinic and was diagnosed with tic douloureux. It (and I quote) "has been known as one of the most painful conditions known to humankind." Edward Munch's painting, "The Scream," is not even close to how it feels.

I was given some pills and told that was about all that I could do for it. They just made me lethargic but otherwise didn't help much except for just kind of made the lead not so intense, but it still felt like a concrete weight was slamming against your face.

For about three months it was awful. I was at a meeting one day when one hit me and I almost fell to the floor. Someone who was visiting that day from another group asked what was wrong when I quit talking and just slumped my head over. I told him and he said his mother had had that, and there was a surgeon in Dallas that was doing a new procedure. He was among only a few in the world that did it.

Judy made the appointment and off we went.

Now the way they would do this surgery is, they would put you under, then stick a long needle under your chin up to your cheek and slowly bring you back to consciousness, then they'd scrape around until they hit the nerve that was randomly exploding. When you screamed they knew they were in the right place. Next, they'd put you back under and scrape the nerve out. After about six times of them doing this, when I was coming to, I tried to tell them I'd changed my mind and to quit, but I couldn't make myself clear.

Unbeknownst* to me, after they were done, the doctor went out and told Judy that they had a hard time getting me under and had to use almost three times the amount of the anesthesia they usually did.

Judy explained: "Well, doc, he's had access to the best dope money can buy for 20 years, so I can understand that."

In 2001 I was walking up the stairs at the Sons Of Herman Hall in Dallas to start my set. A man behind me asks, "how long have you had that limp?"

I don't even turn around but say, "since I flipped a jeep when I was 19. So about 30 years. "

I thought back to the accident.

To get to Middlefork Lake you leave Red River and drive six miles on a two lane gravel road, then you put it in four wheel drive and back up the first switchback, then forward on the next, and then back up the next, and keep backing then going forward for about 10 of them for two or so miles, and you're there. You do this because there isn't enough room to make the turns. You go in a C4 short wheel base jeep.

That morning Rick and I took two C4 jeeps up to the lake with three fishermen in each one and drop them off. When it comes time to pick them up, our boss told me to take a long wheel base C7 jeep and bring all of them down in it.

I didn't think that much about it at the time, but as I was driving up right at switchback eight near this little waterfall, I had some trouble because the jeep was longer than it was supposed to be. I had to do a couple of back and forth turnabouts to get it to back up the right way.

I picked up the fishermen and we headed back down. I got to that same switchback, tried to back it down. The damn jeep slid and leaned over this ledge, tilted awkwardly. The fishermen jumped out and got clear, and the jeep slid off the cliff. I fell about 20 feet, then the jeep falls too, and landed on its side with the front wheel on my legs.

I was pinned beneath the damn thing. There was dust and broken glass and twisted metal and fishing poles and bait and fish and ice chests scattered all around me. I can't feel my legs at all. A bunch of the men climbed down to try to lift the jeep off of me. They couldn't budge it. A TCU football defensive lineman named Robber Swain — who was on the fishing trip — came over and lifted the thing off me by himself(!), then ran down the mountain to get help. Nobody was gonna be coming behind us since we were the last ones at the lake. They leaned me against a tree, but I still couldn't feel my legs.

After a while, a couple of jeeps showed up. They lifted me onto one and we got back to town where they transferred me to another jeep, and we made the 38 mile drive to Taos. I started to feel my legs, and they began to ache.

Nothing was full tilt broken but some ligaments were torn and there were small hip fractures, cuts and bruises. They gave me some crutches and I left.

I returned from that memory to the Sons and got onstage.

That hip had been been hurting for a number of years and for the couple of years previous, I was not able to sleep at night for more than three hours in a row. I continually woke up in pain, fell back asleep, then woke up a few hours later hurting, because now it had deteriorated to bone against bone.

The man went over to Judy at the merch table. He says he is an orthopedic surgeon and he'll fix me so I won't walk like a car with a bent frame whose rear end is trying to pass its front.

Dr. Don Johnston donated his services and MusiCares helped with the rest.

I went under the knife and got a hip replacement. I came to after the operation, and the pain from the surgery was less than the what was there before, so I don't even need the morphine drip they put me on. I did ask if I could get a "to go" bag in case i wanted it later.

I was kidding. I'm pretty sure I was....

Yeah, I was.

So Dr. J.: Thanks for fixing my jalopy.

*The book was finished but I wanted to use the word *unbeknownst* somewhere in it so I added this story here.

No Lie

Written by Ray Wylie Hubbard
Snake Farm Publishing (SESAC)

Savannah she stands in the door, she's lookin' cool and southern
She asks me if I want some, and I said "I can't take another one."
I said "I can't seem to find my stuff, offer some help, I'll except it"
She said "Your guitar's out in the back of the truck where you left it."

It's no lie
It's no lie
It's no lie babe
I got to quit gettin' high

I must have been cursed by a woman at one time
That would explain my luck
I was arrested on the 4th of July, was something about my conduct
When I got out I went downtown to try to find Mr. Foley
He's an ornery son of a bitch but his songs is almost holy
Now Jesus is on the mainline is what Mr. McDowell tells me
When I hear him sing that song, words fail me
Ms. Williams tells me that Jesus turned the water into wine
You'd think somebody could do something like that
Would be a friend of mine

rwh

here is the secret to the universe...okay, maybe not, but it is the thing that actually gave me a career after i was forty two years old. don't tell anybody…ready? *its an E chord without the third...repeat…it's an E chord without the third.*

that's it.

once i got that and i don't recall who taught it to me my life changed…see i had the fingerpicking together but once i learned the E without the third i got rude. it was when i started getting low down and night club smoky cool and knowing i had something going on… it gave these songs like "rabbit" and "snake farm" and "down-home country blues" and "black wings" and so many others a door to come through that wasn't there before.

i was stardust.

i was golden.

well, maybe not but i was at least laying down a nasty groove with a chord that reached into my very soul and whispered, "here you are, brother! wasn't fire, this is what was stolen from the gods and now you is rockin' and now you is rollin' and now you is bluesin' and no matter what else happens in your life…you is dripping cool walking round groovy with the E. the E without the third will honor your love for it."

here's what it is:

open low E, lay first finger on A and D string on the second fret, little finger on the G string on the forth fret, open B string and open high E string.

hear it? feel it? it still makes me shiver when i play it.

okay. to go from the E without the third to an A chord, don't do the first finger on the D string, middle finger on the G string and third finger on the B string on the second fret…just lay your first finger across the D G B strings on the second fret. don't worry if the high E doesn't ring out. you really don't need it to make a statement.

once you learn the E without the third you ain't a wimpy 2% homogenized casper milk toast white bread guitar strummer in a button down shirt no more, baby… now you rock. feel it? can you feel it? play it…hit that chord. hit it…feel it! feel it coming up from your belly? to your throat? coming out the top of your head? feel your ears smiling? play it. play the chord! hear that

E without the third! now believe it! hit that chord... say it with me out loud!!! "yeah...yeah!...ray, i hear it, i hear it ! i'm healed! i'm healed! i believe! i rock, ray, i rock! thank you, ray! thank you! i rock!..i rock"...or if you don't, when you play that chord you'll at least feel this dark sweet coolness surrounding you...a feeling kinda similar to that of smoking a cigarette after your first lowdown dirty backseat sexual encounter with a girl named shirley. anyhow that's how it felt to me.

there it is. the gospel truth...that means good news truth if you're not aware of what gospel means.

oh yeah, there was one thing in the past that i knew for sure was the gospel truth. i mean i believed it was carved in stone somewhere. but i was wrong and it took kitty wells to set me straight by telling me it wasn't God who made honky tonk angels. i coulda swore it was.

anyhow hope that helps as a bunch of people asked me about it...well not a bunch...a few...well there was a guy one time who...okay nobody did, but i had a good time typing this.

Rabbit

Written by Ray Wylie Hubbard
Snake Farm Publishing (SESAC)

Well I saw this old dog was chasing this rabbit
I saw a dog was chasing this rabbit
I saw a dog was chasing this rabbit
It was Sunday about noon
I said to the rabbit "You gonna make it?"
I said to the rabbit "Are you gonna make it?"
I said to the rabbit "You gonna make it"
The rabbit said "Well I got to."

Well a woman's heart's a sacred thing
A woman's heart's a sacred thing
A woman's heart's a sacred thing
So what's a man to do
"Try a little tenderness" Otis Redding said
"Try a little tenderness" is what he said
"Try a little tenderness" Otis said
Then he said "I got to, got to
Good God, watch me work."

There's two kinds of people in the world
There's two kinds of people in the world
There's two kinds of people in the world
The day people and the night people
And it's the night people's job
It's the night people's job
It's the night people's job
To get the day people's money

Well between the devil and the deep blue sea
Between the devil and the deep blue sea
Between the devil and the deep blue sea
That's where I am, I don't know what that means
Maybe it means I'm funky and cool

Maybe it means I'm funky and cool
Maybe it means I'm funky and cool
I seriously doubt if that what if means

"If it's in the groove everybody loves it"
"If it's in the groove everybody loves it"
"If it's in the groove everybody loves it"
Howlin' Wolf said that

We've a short time to be here
We've a short time to be here
We've a short time to be here
So get out of your rut and get in the groove
So get out of your rut and get in the groove
So get out of your rut and get in the groove

chapter 24

Snake Farm, "Sonsabitches," A List

I was going to title my last album for Rounder Records "Contractual Obligation," but I didn't. It's called *Delirium Tremolos*. It's the one Jerry Wexler sent me the postcard congratulating me on — just thought I'd mention how much he liked it again.

I had a bunch of songs and we were getting ready to do another record but didn't know whether to find a new label or to release it ourselves.

We met Jimmy Perkins who was starting a record label called Sustain. He said all the right words to get me to sign. However, the words were flat out lies, and he knew he was lying at the same time he said them. It was a horrible feeling when we found that out. He used the ploy of being "a good Christian family man," and did a lot of talking about principles, morals and caring about the artist to get us to sign.

When we realized he was blatantly dishonoring the contract, we had to lawyer up. The day before he was to appear in court on fraud charges, he settled out of court. His lawyer said Jimmy had told him that he had sent all royalties to the Harry Fox Agency, and we got a fax releasing the rights to *Snake Farm* back to us. After a few weeks, we found out Harry Fox never got the money. Our lawyer called his lawyer and the man was shocked when he found out the truth. He apologized and said he didn't know that Jimmy Perkins was a lying son of a bitch when he was representing him, that he was ashamed of his client for lying to him, and wouldn't have any further dealings with him. We got the rights back. Since the album was still new, it would have cost us more in legal fees than what was owed, so we didn't take it further. We keep the fax and the correspondence in a file labeled "weasels, liars, sonsabitches and thieves." It's not as thick as you would think.

It was disheartening to have this happen after being sober for 15 years. Judy can read people very well and will rarely let a weasel get past her. Robert Earl Keen Jr., Pat Green and Jay Boy Adams had also worked with Perkins and had unfortunate dealings with him too. They called me and thanked me for saying "...it's Jimmy Perkins and the other sonsabitches* who ripped off musicians and stole their riches," in my song "New Year's Eve at the Gates of Hell."

It may not sound like it, but I am over the resentment. I'm just writing historical facts here. If he was on fire I *would* pee on him to put it out.

There is one other thing. Sometimes I get kind of down because it can be frustrating to see some of these young dudes who have tour buses, guitar techs and roadies — all making a bunch of money and getting played all over the radio. The success is one thing; but the real pisser for me is that they think they're good songwriters — they're not.

I feel I have the right to judge the quality of their work because I've seen — and therefore have no choice but to compare them to — Townes Van Zandt or Michael Murphey or B.W. Stevenson or Blaze Foley or Gurf Morlix or James McMurtry or Slaid Cleaves or Hayes Carll or Patty Griffin or Lucinda Williams or Freddie King or Lightnin Hopkins or Mance Lipscomb or Chris Robinson or Guy Clark or Billy Joe Shaver or Bob Dylan or Eric Anderson or Paul Siebel or Stephen Stills or Steve Earle or Tony Joe White or Gary Stewart or Ernest Tubb or Charlie Musselwhite or Stevie Ray Vaughan or Johnny Vandiver or Waylon Jennings or Willie Nelson or Tim Hardin or Joe Walsh or Ringo Starr or Buddy Miller or Roger Tillison or Lisa Mednik or Jerry Jeff Walker or Billy Batson or Johnny Cash or Doug Sahm or Joe Ely or Kevin Welch or Jimmy La Fave or Steve Goodman or Mary Gauthier or John Prine or Butch Hancock or Jimmy Dale Gilmore or Scrappy Jud Newcomb or Troy Campbell or Stephen Bruton or Kris Kristofferson or Eliza Gilkyson, or many other great writers I have seen perform. So the bar is set pretty high. There are some young cats I think that have "the poison of a poet" in their hearts, and write like they have jumped out of an airplane without a parachute, desperate to get it all down before they hit the ground, and have the chops to do it: Jonathan Tyler, Dirty River Boys, Javi Garcia, Will Callers, Crow Black Chicken, Luther Dickinson, Otis Gibbs, Scott H. Biram, Sam Baker, Ray Bonneville, Band Of Heathens, Justin Eady, If Birds Could Fly.

These guys give me hope that all is not lost; I have this dream...and it is that I may keep breathing long enough to live in a post-country-rapping-goofy-dancing-bro'-douchebag-faux-outlaw music era.

*Webster's dictionary defines son of a bitch as a man who is nasty, rude or otherwise offensive. (He lied, he was a thief, he was offensive…no libel case here.)

New Year's Eve at the Gates of Hell

Written by Ray Wylie Hubbard
Snake Farm Publishing (SESAC)

It's New Year's Eve at the gates of hell
Give the Antichrist a cigarette and tell him
The boy's here all the way from Oklahoma
Oh lord what the hell is that aroma?
It's Jimmy Perkins and all the sons-a-bitches
Who ripped off musicians and stole their riches

They're burning over yonder with the Fox News whores
Oh look is that the singer for The Doors
Nope, my mistake cause no matter what they did
Poets deserve to be in heaven and by the way, kid
Why am I here when I wasn't that bad?
I just didn't like churches but I never wore plaid

Now I know I'm funky and strip bar dirty
And I like a Les Paul through a Vox AC30
There's something about a lipstick pickup
Plugged right into a Blond Tremolux
But I guess I deserve to be burned alive
Since I pawned my '59 ES 335

And sure I drank a lot of gin and tonic
But I never threw away my Panasonic
I kept that turntable through my divorce
Playing Neil Young and Crazy Horse
Drunk out of my mind singing "Tonight's The Night"
It was as lethal on vinyl as China White

Now maybe one time I used an Ouija board
And I never learned to make a B flat chord

So I got a double headed snake tattoo
I love Tao Te Ching by Lao Tsu
And the action and the motion of a roulette wheel
And a woman walking away in a pair of high heels

Now once I drew an inside straight flush
And I wished I could sing like Otis Rush
The truth of the matter is I really can't sing
But I can quote Martin Luther King
His words are stronger than angel dust is
"The arc of the moral universe is long but it bends toward justice"

Now back to New Year's Eve at the Gates of Hell
It's kind of like the Beverly Hills Hotel
Before you can get a table next to the fire
A sign says jacket and tie required
The devil is bad and God of course is good
But there's one thing I never understood
God throws us down in hell for all our sins
Burning in a fire and it never ends
The decision is made at the highest level
Seems God out sources his work to the devil
Like he's an employee on the vice squad
Appears like the devil is working for God

chapter 25

Abandoned Log Cabin, Gratitude

We moved to Wimberley when Lucas was four. I found a little stone house toward Dripping Springs. After we'd been there a couple of years, Judy suggested we look to see what else was available.

We found a professional gambler who also did real estate, and drove all around Wimberley for a couple of months. Finally, he said, "what are you looking for?"

I said, "I want a log cabin."

Judy told him, "I want a swimming pool."

"That's weird," he replied. "This log home is going to be on the market in about two weeks. The woman who owned it became ill and her family — who are in the oil business — moved her back to Houston. Her live-in boyfriend came up and stripped the place. It's been abandoned for about four years.

"Let's go look at it," I said

We undid the chain on the driveway, went up this hill, and there it was…it looked like the Munsters or Dracula's or the Texas Chainsaw Massacre people's house. It was overgrown with weeds. The pool was black and green with some fur and bones from some little animal in it that had drowned. Some walls were rotted out, there were no doors, windows were broken, no cabinets, not even a kitchen sink — just two pipes screwed off coming out of the wall. The whole place smelled like mildew.

I got out of the car and said, "I love it."

Judy said, "I ain't living here."

We left and went home. I drove back about eight that evening, parked, crawled over the chain and walked up the hill to the house. I stood on the porch and the sun was setting over what they call the Devil's Backbone and it was a painting from God. I walked to the side and could look down on the town of Wimberley. I have never known such quiet. A fox walked by — walked, didn't run — and I went back to our little house knowing that this was where I wanted to live.

I didn't say anything to Judy about going up there.

The next morning she woke up and said, "I dreamed about that house and we're gonna buy it."

Robin Shivers helped us get a loan and we got it. We left the stove and refrigerator at the house we sold and had $800 left to our name. Judy said, "We can either buy a stove and refrigerator or we can get the pool cleaned."

Since it was July, we spent the money to get the pool cleaned, and all that summer we used an ice chest and a microwave. We tacked up sheets for the doors and used the bathroom sink to wash dishes in until we got one in the kitchen.

Judy learned how to drywall and mud, I learned how to hang doors, and Lucas learned how to swim.

We're still here. We've been here fixing up this place in Wimberley for almost 20 years.

One of the great things about living in a log cabin is that when people come over and say something like, "that door's kinda crooked isn't it?" I tell 'em it's rustic charm.

Sometimes when I think back or reread what I've written here, I wonder how I got from being that barefooted tow-headed kid in Oklahoma, dressed in overalls shooting at wasps with a bb gun, to here on top of a hill in a log cabin looking out the window at a sunset that drips a beautiful crimson over a wild, purple and gold blue yonder.

Then I quit wondering, acknowledge the fact that I have had a spiritual awakening, say "thanks," pick up a Gibson guitar with a 1959 Southern jumbo body that's got a 1949 J45 neck on it, with a Dearmond Toaster Top pickup screwed on it behind the sound hole, plug it into an Alan Durham Sex Drive pedal and then into a 1959 Fender Vibrolux Tweed amp, hit an E chord without the third, think about my family and friends, and my gratitude is far higher than my expectations ever were.

Lazarus

Written by Ray Wylie Hubbard
Snake Farm Publishing (SESAC)

So here we are now, guitars and drums
High and lowdown just some dharma bums
Gatemouth would tell you rehearsal's overrated
Baptists will tell you it's all predestinated

Between the devil and God
Between the first breath and last
Somewhere under heaven
With no future and a hell of a past
We in the mud and scum of things, moaning, crying, lying
At least we ain't Lazarus who had to think twice about dying
At least we ain't Lazarus who had to think twice about dying

So here we are now, still preceding grace
We ain't easy to look at and keep a straight face
Inspired by Rimbaud, ain't angelic
Influenced by the dead, just gets you psychedelic

So here we are now kinda like abandoned dogs
Wrapped up in gunnysacks and singing cast iron songs
We're weird old America grinning with sharp teeth
We're beautiful on the surface and rotten underneath

chapter 26

The Equation, The Whole Cosmic Shebang, The End

Okay, I've written all I'm gonna write, so the book's over and it has been fun...well there was some anguish here and there every now and then, but mostly I enjoyed writing it.

Like right there.

For a few minutes I debated in my old head whether I should use "hither and yon" as it would appear more literaturary than "here and there"...and then of course there is no such word as "literaturary," so then I have to go back and correct autocorrect to get that word in here.

Anyway...I want to leave you with this and it might be redundant from an earlier piece I wrote, but as they say, "repetition strengthens and confirms."

So here's what I've learned about songwriting and I guess about life too. One day I decided to write it down and it looks like a formula or an equation or some science fair project thrown together at the last minute by a third grader the night before it was due at school the next day.

Anyhow, here it is:

Inspiration + Craft x Time & Effort – Fear & Doubt
+ Purpose = Properous Songwriter.

Here's what it means.

INSPIRATION

One of my favorite quotes is from Flannery O'Connor: "Never second guess inspiration."

I would add that it is okay to rewrite. Inspiration is what songwriters call the "great aha!"

'Aha! That would be a good idea for a song.'

They can come from anywhere and I ought to know: A wasp's nest, a snake farm, a Greek myth, a coricidin bottle, a redneck mother, an Ace Reed cartoon, a stripper and / or a Les Paul. These are all songs I have written in case you didn't know. So whatever it is, it could be a song if we just become mindful, knowing this creative spark could ignite at any moment. I recommend the books, *As A Man Thinketh,* by James Allen and Rainer Maria Rilke's *Letters To A Young Poet* as they are filled with incredibly powerful, enlightening stuff. Also Sylvie Simmons' *I'm Your Man* is also an inspiring read.

+ CRAFT

It means knowing what you're doing, learning and studying songs. I would add learning and studying great songs (as opposed to, you know, crap songs). Knowing what kind of song it's going to be: Whether it's a 12 bar blues, a folk ballad, rocking low down, dirty roots rock and roll…the structure of them, verse-chorus-verse-chorus-bridge-verse-chorus or just verse, verse, verse. Sheila Davis's *The Craft of Lyric Writing* is a good place to start.

x TIME AND EFFORT

Gonna have to do it. The more time and effort, the better you get.

I spent hours upon hours counting 'one and two and three and four and' while my right thumb and three fingers thumped and plucked on them old EADGBE stings...and then...and then...I put a piece of glass on the third finger of my left hand and… and…aghhhhh!!!! It's alive! It's alive! the monster lives!!!! A creature runs wild among us!!! sliiiiddde guitar…okay…maybe a little overboard, but man, it means a lot to me to be able to do the slide guitar thing.

– FEAR AND DOUBT

These are the things that limit us. If we can remove our fear and doubt, it is unlimited what we can become.

I remember a line in Rilke's *Letters To A Young Poet* — and I'm paraphrasing — but basically it says, our fears are like dragons guarding our most precious treasure.

In my case, I asked God to remove my fear, called up Sam Swank in Dallas and asked him if he would teach me how to fingerpick. He said yeah, and I went and learned a few patterns, and the first song I wrote after that was "The Messenger."

Now doubt has plagued me a lot throughout my life. I guess I felt inadequate when we moved from Soper to Dallas when I was in the fourth grade. I was used to overalls and going barefooted and playing with frogs. Then I was in this huge city and 500 kids in one school and I did not fit in. I was made fun of and the kids called me a rube. I was one but I didn't like being called that. Now in Oklahoma, we settled our arguments by wrestling like young Abraham Lincoln; but at John H. Reagan School for Young Hoodlum Boys, the kids just came up and hit you in the face with a fist. I had many bloody noses throughout the fourth grade. My dad pulled some strings, somehow, and got me transferred to Rosemont Elementary where he taught sixth grade history and english. It was a more affluent school with rich kids, so I was really out of place there, too.

Anyhow, back to the formula thing concerning doubt. If you doubt and think that your song isn't very good, well don't. Whenever you have any doubts about what you're writing, like, maybe this song isn't any good, then the next thought should be, "where's the proof?" There is none. It's only our own heads messing with us. Just listen to the fucking radio. Anyone with even a little knowledge of the blues, folk music, the pentatonic scale, and a soul can write a better song than a desperate-to-get-a-cut-must-be-approved-by-a-A&R-Top-40-record-executive-cookie-cutter-got-a-publishing-deal-briefcase-cliched Nashville songwriter.

I prefer the scruffy poet kind: those that are condemned by the gods to write. Those who tear off a fragment of their soul and make it rhyme and fit the laws of music. Those who write not thinking about the future of what they write. Those who write 'cause they got no choice…the badass walking cool literate song writing sonsabitches; and just so you know…there are badass walking cool literate song writing women sonsabitches, too.

+ PURPOSE

A quote I love (and my friend Thom Jurek knew who said it, I didn't) by Benjamin E. Mays is: "The tragedy of life doesn't lie in not reaching your goal. The tragedy lies in having no goal to reach."

So let's set a goal: Prosperous songwriter. Now that doesn't mean I have a Mercedes in my garage. I don't. I don't even have a garage. Prosperous to me means that I can do what I love to do and I can pay my bills.

Ok, let's look deeper and get into some metaphysical-spiritual-badass-mumbo-jumbo kind of juju to get your mojo working.

Let's assume for a minute that the purpose of the universe, since the beginning of time, is to contribute to life. Whether it was created in six days or the big bang banged, or a turtle burped the universe out, human beings came into existence, and some energy within the universe has contributed to improving us.

One way to look at this is that the purpose of the universe is to contribute to life. We should make that *our* purpose. It's not what can we get it's what we can give. By doing that, we align ourselves with the purpose of the universe. So our purpose in writing songs is to improve people's lives whether it is making them smile, giving them a groove to dance to, inspiring them to sing along or maybe create some lyrics that can make them forget for a few moments that some darkness has swooped down on them and got them troubled.

The reason we are here is the same reason the universe is here: To contribute. Somehow, by that simple shift of thought by making a commitment and taking the action, amazing things happen. So let's look at this whole picture.

We set a goal or goals. We look at the things we have going for us. We look at the things we need to do. We put forth the time and effort and do them. We ask God to remove our fear and doubt. (Even if you don't believe in God, do it anyway. God doesn't really need to hear your prayers, so look at it as an action to show resolution.) And now, since we have the same purpose as the universe there is nobody or nothing against us. You say, "What about the Devil, Ray? Huh? What about him trying to keep us from being successful?"

Hey, the Devil digs a groove. And as my friend Gurf Morlix said, "A lot of people sold their soul to the Devil...can't none of 'em play like Robert Johnson." So if you should make a bargain with the Devil, make sure you get the "play the guitar like Robert Johnson" deal. But you really don't have to do that...just practice, practice, practice, and then practice some more.

= PROSPEROUS SONGWRITER

So now if we are putting forth the time and effort learning the craft and aligning it with inspiration and writing without fear and doubt, and our purpose is noble in alliance with the Whole Cosmic Energy shebang underlying the material world and life its very self and there is nothing whatsoever against us...well, then it's only a matter of time until we reach our goal.

Reread the above paragraph again so I don't have to type it again. Believe it as if your very life depends on it. Mine did.

When I was 41 years old I was playing at Charlie's Airport Lounge starting at 10 p.m. alternating three sets a night with a lingerie show. Charlie's opened at seven in in the morning, and some of the clientele — and a few of the models — usually had been there drinking from the moment the door was unlocked for business. They were not Victoria's Secret models with big old white wings on a runway somewhere — these gals were not aging gracefully — and I don't like to judge — but unless they found the Lord or a nearsighted desperate man, this was probably their last go-round before becoming hookers at some truck stop south of Waco. Hmm, wow. I guess I do like to judge. Sorry. I'll work on that. Well anyhow it was not a great gig. It was also very disheartening to see a bunch of goobers with guitars that were metaphorically deficient rolling to sold-out gigs in big fancy tour busses and jumping around on TV and rolling in dough.

After one demoralizing night, I went home and meditated. After my thoughts quit racing and kind of smoothed out, I opened my eyes and made a commitment to respect whatever creative spark was within me and no matter what, I was going to write songs without compromise and align my purpose with some energy that I believed honored my faith in it to do what I thought would be beneficial to the other human beings walking around on the planet.

In January of 2013, someone asked me if at the age of 66 didn't I think I was a little old to be making my first appearance on *Late Night with David Letterman*.

I said I didn't want to peak too soon.

Stone Blind Horses

Written by Ray Wylie Hubbard
Snake Farm Publishing (SESAC)

There are some saints that have been forgotten
Like most of my drunken prayers
They say there's a heaven and it's above the yonder
Where there's no more crosses to bear

There's ghosts along the highways
And there's storms out on the seas
My only hope is somewhere in that heaven
Someone is saying a prayer for me

The high slurred whistle of a red winged blackbird
Sounds like he's singing "Oh that I might die"
It's a song for those that have fallen
Unrepentant and no more alibis

I been riding stone blind horses
Never seeing a reason to believe
Hey sweet Genevieve, say a prayer for me.
And the wild young cowboys, old drunks
Paramours and thieves

afterword

the cake is done, here's the icing…

Enlightenment, Endarkenment, Resurrection and Redneck Mother Love

by Judy Hubbard

(First printed in *Lone Star Music Magazine* in 2011)

It's 6:30 a.m. on July 30, 2011, somewhere in Massachusetts, and I can't sleep, wondering why they call this place the Quality Inn. Maybe in some foreign language "quality" means "dump." But the venue paid for it, so I can't really complain. Instead, I recall a pearl of wisdom that was shared with me years earlier: "Keep your level of gratitude higher than your expectations." God knows I've slept in worse. Besides, in a few hours we begin the pilgrimage to my own personal mythical motherland: Woodstock, N.Y., where my husband, Ray Wylie Hubbard, will play a show at Levon Helm's Barn. I am beyond grateful ....

The story really begins in 1964, when I was seven years old and sitting two feet away from my family's black-and-white television set. The Beatles were about to make history with their first live television performance in the U.S.A. on *The Ed Sullivan Show*. I needed to be close enough to kiss Ringo. He was my Beatle.

Music affects each of us in different ways. To some it is mere background noise; to others, a mood enhancer; many consider it the soundtrack to their lives. To me, it was a doorway to freedom, salvation — a respite from the chaos which was my life.

Here's the Cliff's Notes version: Dallas, Texas; five kids; Catholic schools; she hated me; he was never home; secrets; rage; and guns — lots of guns. In my childhood home there was a gun under every chair. My father wore a shoulder holster (and no, he wasn't in law enforcement). Bless his heart, he is 84 and still packs a .38 every time he leaves the house. It wasn't normal, but I didn't know that at the time. Shit was going on that you didn't talk about to anybody; the code was, "Keep your mouth shut." So music became my escape. I could hide in my room, spin my records, put on headphones to tune out the noise, and dream of the day when I'd be old enough to leave my house of horrors.

The Beatles were my introduction. I was lucky, as the next 10 years brought me — and everybody else, whether they admit it or not — some of the greatest musical transformations in history. Rock, folk, country, blues, soul. The Band, the Byrds, Janis Joplin, Jimi Hendrix, Otis Redding, Donovan, Creedence Clearwater Revival, Bob Dylan, the Who, the Rolling Stones... they each had their own identity. I loved it all. By the end of the decade, songwriters were writing poetic tomes of social protest, giving the young generation a voice of its own. Folk and rock were crossing into each other's territories. The musical education was plentiful, available, and all but unavoidable for anyone remotely interested. Me, I yearned for it.

It was 1969. I was 12. Plans were underway for a music festival to take place over three days on a farm in upstate New York. The festival was to be forever known as Woodstock. For me, records were no longer enough, I needed to experience the music live. I fought with my parents about it for weeks but there was no way they were going to let me go. As a parent I can look back and laugh at my unrealistic request (although I would have taken my son Lucas!) But at the time, I was devastated. So I found solace with my new friends — Marlboro Reds, Everclear and weed — and continued to dream of the great escape.

As it turns out, I didn't have to go very far. By the early '70s, the homegrown "Texas Music Scene" was already beginning to be recognized on a national level in magazines such as *Rolling Stone* and *Billboard*. Though "Texas" and "music" had long been synonymous, the sound coming out of the Lone Star State lacked a definitive description. Detroit was known for Motown, Memphis had Stax, New Orleans had funky R&B and Cajun, Nashville had country, but nowhere else but Texas could you find all of the above plus rock, Tex-Mex, folk and the blues all combined within the borders of one state (or in the case of *Rolling Stone* cover boy Doug Sahm, within a single artist.) At first, Texas country rebels like Willie Nelson and Waylon Jennings were kept at arms' length by the music industry status quo, especially in Nashville; but once their freeform style of country music (alternately called "progressive," "outlaw" and even "country rock") took off back home, it was only a matter of time before Willie, Waylon and a host of others were making records on their own terms.

Early on in that cosmic cowboy boom period, Willie was throwing an outdoor music festival in his hometown of Abbott, Texas. This time I decided it would be better to ask forgiveness than permission, so a girlfriend and I ran away from home and headed to the big to-do. The repercussions I faced once I came back home the next day were worth it. Listening to songs over and over on a record player or on the radio was an important experience for me; but seeing the artist perform those songs live was not only more immediate, it was life-changing. The music went on all day, with artists frequently joining one another onstage. Willie called up a young songwriter to join him on a song and introduced him as Ray Wylie Hubbard. He was cute, outlaw, and oozed cool. Years later my girlfriend recounted to me that from that day on, every time we attended a show that Ray played, as soon as his set was over, I would turn to her and say, "One of these days, I'm gonna marry that Ray Wylie Hubbard." One thing was certain: I had found my people. I was home. It was 1973. I was 16.

From that day forward anytime there was a music festival in Texas, I was there. In between festivals I would head to venues like the Armadillo in Austin or the Texas Tea House and Mother Blue's in Dallas. Wherever Texas bands were playing, I went.

Returning home after one such event, my mother handed me an empty pillowcase with instructions to fill it with whatever belongings of mine would fit, and be out of her house for good in 20 minutes. It was non-negotiable. So with my new freedom, and the wisdom of a 16 year old, I left. To this day I've never spent a night in their house. I wasn't quite prepared to be on my own, but I was ready. I had no idea how to go to a job interview, open a checking account or cook, but hey, I had skills: I could shoot a bird off a telephone wire from a moving car, run a casino out of a garage, and roll a joint with one hand.

A friend who was in his early 20s and had a house of his own took me in. In exchange for room and board, I was to feed the animals, keep the place tidy, the fridge full, and bullets stocked in the three re-loaders he had set up in the gun room. In exchange, I got my own room (complete with a waterbed which had a holster and small caliber gun attached to the back of the headboard), access to the drug box, and food. Other roommates would move into the house over the years. One played football for the Dallas Cowboys, while another was a world champion drag racer. It wasn't a bad deal.

I soon landed a job at Mother Blue's as the door girl working until close. Then I'd hang after hours, when the staff and musicians would gather around drinking and telling road stories. Occasionally I would work the after-hours poker games upstairs serving drinks. It wasn't unusual for a game to include Freddie King, Bugs Henderson, Steve Fromolz and Eric Clapton. Some of the regulars who played the venue were King, Lightnin' Hopkins, Willis Alan Ramsey, Rusty Wier, Howlin' Wolf, Townes Van Zandt and B.W. Stevenson. Next door was a sister club, which brought in rock bands and stayed opened until 4 a.m. They became legendary due to the musicians who would drop by after playing arena shows in town: Alice Cooper, David Bowie, Robert Plant and Frank Zappa were just a few of the many artists who came in to relax, hang out, and listen to music.

One memorable night, a young songwriter playing the club asked me to go out after his show to see a band playing across town. We went to Fannie Ann's and saw Ray Wylie Hubbard and the Cowboy Twinkies. My date joined them onstage for a song and we hung around after the show so the two could meet. It was the first time I actually met Ray. It was the first time Ray met Jimmy Buffet.

There was a price to pay for my youth, however. I had quit school, and my drinking and drug use continued to escalate. By 1975 it was out of control; I was drinking almost daily and was shooting heroin to feed my addiction. I eventually left the club in hopes that a regular day job would slow me down. It didn't. I had averaged three trips a year to jail since I was 16 for drugs, fighting or driving crooked. Henry Wade, the District Attorney in Dallas, sat me in his office and told me it was over. None of my trading on family connections could get me out of the next scrape — he was revoking my get-out-of-jail card. It was my wakeup call. I felt like an old woman and I was tired. It was 1980. I was 22.

Living without drinking and getting high meant a total shift in my playmates and playgrounds. Although it doesn't bother me at all to be around people drinking now, at first it was too difficult, so I stayed out of the bars and only went to an occasional concert. The movie *Urban Cowboy* had just come out, turning my two-stepping honky-tonks into country discos. John Lennon had been murdered, and hippies around the world were in mourning. I didn't much feel like partying anyway. I had gotten a job in the car business and worked all the time. And twice a month, I would drive to the women's prison in Gatesville, where I volunteered in a program for women in recovery. Trust me, that'll keep you sober. It did me.

One night a friend asked me to go with a group to Poor David's Pub in Dallas to see Ray Wylie. It was 1988, and I hadn't seen or heard anything about him since the late-70s. He was funny, wore Cuban heels on his cowboy boots and looked even more like an outlaw than he did at that Willie festival back in '73, but he was also sober — and his songs melted me. There was an eerie feeling that came over me, like I had been in love with him in another life. I couldn't explain it but it was strong. After the show I hung out by the green room door waiting for him to come out. We chatted a bit and he asked me to come to his show the next night. Six months later, we were married. It was 1989. I was 31. We are still inseparable.

When Ray and I married, his music career wasn't exactly on the front burner, and he wasn't setting the world on fire. He simply played wherever and whenever he could. And while I had always been a music fan and had worked at a live music venue, that hardly qualified me to manage my husband's career. That said, the simple fact was also that it wasn't in my nature to not do anything about it, either.

By the time our wedding day rolled around I had helped out with a few contracts here and there, and began piecing together his history. I came to understand all too clearly that there were no plans for the future! So I came up with a plan: I had four days off from my job and intended to make good use of them, so I booked our honeymoon in Nashville. We would get married, fly to Nashville and stay at the Opryland Hotel, because one of my customers at the Lincoln Dealership was a VP and comped us the room as a wedding present. And while we were there, we'd hit Music Row and simply pick out our favorite record deal. I just knew that once these label execs heard Ray's songs, they too would swoon and jump right on board, and then I could start looking for a sparkly red dress for all those award shows we would attend.

A story of such naiveté would be funny if it wasn't dead on true! But this is how our Honeymoon really unfolded: While we were there, Nashville was hit by a rainstorm followed by a sleet storm followed by more rain. There were no doors open on Music Row, and the few phone calls we made to someone at a label — "a friend of a friend" who said they could get us in the door — all ended in the same polite "thank you; but no thank you."

The best news of the whole trip was the giant food basket sent to our room as a wedding gift, because we were out of money by the third day and were hungry. But hey, I was in love, and Ray was grateful to have someone who believed in him — even if it was an uneducated used-car saleswoman with no music business experience.

He had no label, no manager, and no booking agent. He hadn't released a new record in years. He was booking gigs at places where, before he'd gotten clean, he had previously been paid in booze and cocaine; places that hired bouncers with names like "Shit" and "Doodoo." I remember delivering a new Lincoln to a customer at his office one day. As he was congratulating me on my recent marriage to "that country star," I glanced out the window in his office. The marquee across the street read: "Lingerie Show at 10:00, Ray Wylie Hubbard at 11:00!"

It was around this time I took over Ray's booking. I made a list of all the clubs he had played the last couple of years and starting calling them. How different could this be than what I did at the car dealership all day? I worked in sales and leasing, but not walk-in customers; only referrals or customers I cold called. I was organized, knew how to follow up, and figured it would be a no brainer. On one of my first calls, a club owner told me the last time Ray played, he fell into the drums drunk, and would not be playing there again. Ray explained that it was not uncommon for them to confuse the "three-name guys," and that must have been Jerry Jeff Walker, not him. "Well, that makes sense," I thought, so I went back to smiling and dialing. The next one told me, "No way, he didn't show up the last time we booked him." I explained that it must have been one of those other three-name guys like David Allan Coe or Gary P. Nunn, as people often mix them up. "Well ask his band," the club owner replied, "because they did show up!" Then he hung up.

There were no courses in what I was undertaking at the junior college, no books at the library, and certainly no one to show you the ropes. I had to make it up as I went along, as many in this position do. I went to every gig, as there were no roadies and Ray carried his own sound system. I would help with load in and out and collected the money at the end of the night. I still carried a gun, which was an asset at some of the honky-tonks he was playing at the time. One club owner in Dallas was notorious for shorting bands at the end of the night. He also had a reputation for being coked up, drunk, and a bully. The band waited in the parking lot (really!) while I went upstairs to settle up. He started in with the "you didn't draw and I lost money" bit, setting me up to get stiffed. I wasn't in the mood for him. I had just helped schlep the sound system down a flight of stairs in his shitty cowboy disco, sat through three one-hour sets telling one whiskey-breath dude after the next that I was not sitting alone because I was looking for love but rather because I was "with the band." On top of all that I had to be at work at 8:30 in the morning and we needed the money! He pulled out a revolver and set it on the desk and continued to berate me. I pulled out my Walther PPK/S 9mm and set it on the desk and kept my mouth shut. Whatever my father's parenting skills may have lacked, they made up for in dealing with situations like this. He taught me to never blink first and always use hollow point bullets. We got paid — which I'm sure had a lot to do with the guy thinking that the $500 he owed us was worth it just to make Ray's heat-packing psycho wife with the bad bleach job go away.

Little by little things moved forward. There were others out there who saw what I did in Ray and were willing to give him a chance. In 1992 we released his first CD, *Lost Train of Thought*, on our own. We had local distribution and sold it at gigs. A couple of years later he signed with a small independent label based in Austin and released *Loco Gringo's Lament*. I was pregnant with Lucas at the time and still working at the car dealership while handling all the management and booking. When Lucas was born we hired a girl who was just starting a booking agency and was willing to take on Ray as a client. We moved to Poetry, Texas, which added an hour commute each way to my day job. It was incredibly hard doing everything ourselves, but we tried to remain grateful as we had our own little house on four acres in the country, our little hippie family and a belief that we were on the right path. Neither of us had family to babysit Lucas and it was still necessary for me to work the gigs so we took him with us. Recently, as I watched my now teenaged son playing lead guitar with his dad at a Gruene Hall show, I wondered if he remembered the many nights he slept in the T-shirt box next to me at the merch table at that same club.

In 1997, Auto Nation bought the Lincoln dealership I had worked at for the previous 17 years. I had a good deal going there; they were tolerant of me conducting music business out of my office and basically left me alone. But it was clear all that would change once the new corporation took over. I had never thought about what I would do if I didn't work there. It had been my safety net when I got clean and sober. Our ultimate goal was for me to eventually be able to manage the business without having to work a day job, but we weren't there yet. I didn't exactly have a great resume, with no high school diploma, much less a college one. Hell, with my police record, I couldn't get a job as a WalMart greeter. I was terrified. Still, I called Ray and asked him what he would want to do if I quit my job.

"Move to Wimberley," he said.

Lack of a formal education has been one of the few regrets I carry from my wasted youth. Could I have done a better job managing Ray if I had a college degree? Would I not live in such fear at the prospect of having to compete in the job market should I ever need to? I don't know the answer to those questions. What I do know now is that an abundance of information is available on every aspect of the music business — if you really make an effort to find it. Once we were settled in Wimberley I began to study as if my livelihood depended on it. I joined industry organizations which offered networking and education. I scoured books and researched everything I could find on the Internet about publishing, management, recording contracts, publicity, social media, licensing for TV and film, and running an independent record label. I learned how to create a business plan, how to set realistic goals and work towards them. I subscribe to numerous music-industry dailies in order to stay current on trends, laws, and opportunities in the business. Each January, we review our progress and set new goals.

For many years I believed it was all about the record deal: If we could just get a record deal, success would follow. Or, if we could get with the right publisher, we would automatically start landing cuts on other artists' records. Or, if we could get Ray on this festival, or an opportunity to open for that band on the road, then the rest of the world would see and love him, too. I have since learned it is not that black-and-white, that each artist follows a different path and finding your own is half the battle. Over the years we have re-secured the rights to several of Ray's old songs as well as three of his albums. We filed a lawsuit against a sleazy record label owner and won. We negotiated and sold rights to a screenplay Ray co-wrote which is now a feature film and includes four of his songs. Last year, we set up our own label, Bordello Records, and ran a successful release campaign, garnering a No. 1 spot on the Americana Chart as well as three nominations at the Americana Awards. And although he wasn't happy with the final production of the aforementioned film and the nominations didn't result in a win, I am reminded that getting to either one of those places without the help or backing of a major studio or record label is indeed quite an accomplishment.

I continue to redefine my idea of what "success" is. It is certainly not what it was 23 years ago in a rainy Nashville hotel on my honeymoon. Do we have a fleet of tour buses, Grammys on the wall or sell out Billy Bob's? Do I run with the hip crowd in the Texas music scene, vacation in Hawaii or have an entourage reminding me how great I am? Not even close. What I do have is 31 years without booze or drugs. I have a log home in the Hill Country where the sunset view on our front porch will take your breath away. I have a son starting college in the fall — a son who has never seen the inside of a jail cell and who has grown up loved and secure in the knowledge that no matter what he does, his parents will never throw him away. I have a husband who after 23 years still causes my heart to melt when he straps on his guitar, who continues to reinvent himself as an artist and who has added "screenwriter" and "record producer" to his list of accomplishments. A husband who also now gets phone calls from people like Joe Walsh and Ringo Starr (who I still think of as my Beatle), inviting him to co-write, tour and just hang at their homes. And a husband who generously shares his knowledge with younger artists who look up to him.

Of course, there are days when one disappointment or another leaves me wondering if I'd be better off selling used cars again. But then, without fail, an email will come in. It will be from a bereaved father, recounting the first Ray Wylie Hubbard show he brought his son to 10 years ago and how they continued to attend concerts and share CDs until his son's recent death — explaining that he just wanted to say thank you for the memories. Or it might be from a songwriter who has gone three days clean and sober and looks to Ray as an example of how to navigate this business without drinking. Or a young gal who loves "all things Red Dirt" and thinks "Ray Wylie is cool as shit!" Reading those emails, I am reminded of not only who brought us this far, but who continues to carry us when we want to give up.

We just finished playing the last song to a sold-out crowd at Levon Helm's Barn in Woodstock. He invited Ray up to sing "The Weight" with him and his band, and asked our drummer, Rick Richards, to join him on drums. When the crowd cleared out and Helm's band had all gone home, we joined him at his house to say our goodbyes. As we sat around his kitchen table laughing and telling road stories, I was once more acutely aware of how blessed my life has turned out to be. I really did end up marrying that Ray Wylie Hubbard guy. We have a son whose very existence makes my world a better place. And I finally made it to Woodstock. It was everything I had dreamed it would be.

thom jurek

is a cultural critic, journalist and poet from Detroit. He is a staff writer at *allmusic.com* and former senior editor of the city's news and arts weekly, the *Metro Times*. His reviews, essays and fiction have appeared in various magazines, journals and anthologies. He is the author of *Dub* and *Memory Bags*.

rwh

+ "Music Book Smudge, Country Music Stain"